College Degrees

You Can Earn

From Home

College
Degrees
You Can Earn
From Home

How to Earn a First-Class
Degree Without Attending Class

The New Careers Center, Inc.
with Judith Frey

Live Oak Publications
Boulder, Colorado

Live Oak Publications
PO Box 2193
Boulder, CO 80306
(303) 447-1087
Distributed by Publishers Group West

Library of Congress Cataloging-in-Publication Data
College degrees you can earn from home: how to earn a first-class degree withouth attending class/the New Careers Center, Inc., with Judith Frey.
    p. cm.
Includes index.
ISBN 0-911781-12-9: $14.95
1. Degrees, Academic. 2. College credits. 3. Correspondence schools and courses—Directories. 4. Independent study. I. Frey, Judith. II. New Careers Center, Inc.
LB2381.C65 1995
378.24--dc20

Disclaimer

Every attempt has been made to make this book as accurate and complete as possible. There may be mistakes of content or typography, however, and the author and publisher make no guarantees, warranties, or representations of any kind. This book is designed as a general guide to the subject. The reader is urged to investigate and verify information and its applicability under any particular situation or circumstances.

The author and publisher shall have no liability or responsibility to anyone with respect to contacts, negotiations, or agreements that may result from information in this book, or for any loss or damage caused or alleged to have been caused directly or indirectly by such information. If legal advice or other expert assistance is required, the services of a competent professional person should be sought.

TABLE OF
CONTENTS

Part 1
Earning a College Degree Through Home Study 1

College Degrees That Can Be Earned Through Distance
Study 3
Accreditation 4
Getting Started 6
Types of Courses You Can Take Through Distance Study 6
Getting Academic Credit For Things Your Already Know...........8
Taking Equivalency Examinations 12
Transfer Credit 14
The Regents Credit Bank 15

Part 2
Program Profiles 17
Descriptions of 112 home-study programs, with contact informa-
tion, degrees offered, fees, accreditation, residency requirements
(if any) and other information

Part 3
Index 173

Part 1
Earning a College Degree Through Home Study

If you're thinking of going back to school by means of home study, then congratulate yourself! Furthering your education will increase your earning potential, heighten your satisfaction in work, give you added prestige in society and more self-esteem as an individual.

But does home study actually give you the same education that you would receive attending regular college classes? The American Council on Education compared students who have received credit for extrainstitutional learning with regular on-campus college students: "Recent data showed that their overall performance, in terms of GPA, was higher than that of the student body as a whole; the average number of credits carried each semester was equivalent to the average number carried by the student body as a whole; they were enrolled in all academic departments of the college, etc."

The field of home study, or "distance learning," encompasses taking correspondence courses, earning course credit simply by taking an examination, compiling a portfolio of previous life and work experiences to be assessed for credit, transferring academic credit from other institutions, and receiving college credit for non-academic courses offered by businesses, the government, the military, various associations, and trade unions.

There is a trend in higher education to focus more on the needs of adult non-traditional students—people whose lives make it impossible for them to attend conventional on-campus classes. Colleges and universities have been developing new and better programs that make it easier for adults to study at home, without limiting their personal commitments to work, family, or other activities. Many schools now offer guided independent study programs that allow

1

students to study completely at their own pace.

The whole field of distance education is changing rapidly, as technology provides more and newer methods of offering classroom instruction at the student's location and schedule. Courses are now being offered over cable television or via satellite. Some courses of study supply videotapes of live classroom lectures. Many courses are now being offered by computer technology that can link a home computer with the university computer.

Along with the trend toward greater freedom of time and place, there is increasing recognition in higher education of the real-life needs of non-traditional students—adults who are in mid-career—and degree programs are being offered with more flexible options than ever before. Courses of study are being designed by individual students, with assistance from faculty members, to integrate theory and academic learning with practical projects and on-the-job activities.

The advantages of distance learning go beyond the obvious ones of being able to study whenever and wherever a person chooses—of being able to pursue a college degree while maintaining other lifestyle commitments. Another advantage that is becoming more apparent as schools increasingly structure their programs around the needs and interests of individual students has to do with the quality of education itself. There is evidence that distance learning students actually learn more than their conventional college counterparts. Here's why:

There is more one-to-one interaction with the instructor. Through toll-free telephone lines, fax, and computer access, students may contact their professors at any time with questions or comments and receive back personalized answers—to a greater degree than usually happens in normal classroom settings.

In interactive computer or teleconference class settings—which are increasingly being offered as methods whereby distance-learning students may take part in either live or asynchronous group discussions—it has been shown that students participate more actively than in regular classroom situations. Students respond, ask questions, and volunteer comments more often than their on-campus counterparts.

Motivation is more important—the student is responsible for doing independent study and research. This allows a student to spend more time pursuing topics of special interest without worrying about meeting regular class deadlines. A student may be creative, innovative, and self-directed.

Because of the growing trend in distance education to allow the student to design an individual program of study around career or personal interests, the focus of learning is more relevant and practical. Because of the many options that exist now for receiving college credit for experiential learning from life and work activities, many students are achieving their degree goals in a much shorter time than expected.

COLLEGE DEGREES THAT CAN BE EARNED THROUGH DISTANCE STUDY

Virtually all of the major undergraduate and graduate degree programs currently being offered at colleges and universities may be earned through distance study. The following is a description of the kinds of degrees offered:

ASSOCIATE DEGREES
Most commonly awarded: Associate in Arts (A.A.), Associate in Science (A.S.)

The Associate degree is a two-year undergraduate degree. It is awarded upon completion of a two-year community college program or vocational or technical course. Increasingly, it is being offered by traditional four-year colleges to students who only complete two years (or the equivalent in distance study). There are many different kinds of associate degrees, ranging from Associate in Specialized Technology (A.S.T.), to Associate in Independent Studies (A.I.S.).

BACHELOR'S DEGREES
Most commonly awarded: Bachelor of Arts (B.A.), Bachelor of Science (B.S.)

Although there is no longer a prescribed curriculum for a bachelor's degree, the programs are almost all based on completion of four years of study in a conventional university setting (or its non-traditional equivalent). There are many different kinds of this degree, including Bachelor of Business Administration (B.B.A.), Bachelor of Fine Arts (B.F.A.), Bachelor of Independent Studies (B.I.S.), Bachelor of Education (B.Ed.), and Bachelor of Science in Electronic Engineering (B.S.E.E.).

MASTER'S DEGREES
Most commonly awarded: Master of Arts (M.A.), Master of Science

3

(M.S.)

The master's degree is recognized as the first graduate degree in both academic and professional fields. Traditionally, It takes one to two years of study to complete. Some master's degrees are considered to be professional degrees and stand on their own, while others are mainly preparation for a doctorate and involve some original research and the writing of a thesis. The many kinds of master's degrees parallel the different types of bachelor's degrees, including Master of Public Administration (M.P.A.), Master of Engineering (M.Eng.), Master of Library Science (M.L.S.), and Master of Science in Taxation (M.S.Tax).

DOCTORATE DEGREES

Most commonly awarded: Doctor of Philosophy (Ph.D.), Doctor of Education (Ed.D.), Juris Doctor (J.D.)

Currently the highest graduate degree awarded, requiring up to six or seven years of study in a conventional academic setting (or its non-traditional equivalent). The Doctor of Philosophy is awarded in many academic fields. The Ph.D. degree usually requires original research and the preparation of a written dissertation. A doctorate in education requires the demonstrated ability to do applied research; the Juris Doctor the capacity for legal reasoning.

PROFESSIONAL CERTIFICATE AND PARAPROFESSIONAL PROGRAMS

Examples: Certificate in Computer Science, Paralegal Document, Certificate in Basic Health Care Administration, certificates in various forms of health-related therapy

Credentials for many professions may be earned by means of certificate programs that verify the attainment of a certain level of professional competence.

ACCREDITATION

Most of the schools listed in this book are accredited by one of the six regional accrediting agencies that are recognized by the U.S. Department of Education. In addition, many individual departments within schools are accredited separately by the accrediting body in the specialized field. For example, nursing programs are accredited separately by the National League for Nursing, and clinical psychology programs receive accreditation by the American Psychological Association. The National Home Study Council, which is listed by the

U.S. Department of Education as a nationally recognized accrediting agency, is the only agency responsible for schools anywhere in the United States. (National Home Study Council, 1601 18th Street N.W., Washington, DC 20009 (202) 234-5100)
Here are the six regional accrediting agencies:

Middle States Association of Colleges and Schools
Commission on Higher Education
3624 Market Street
Philadelphia, PA 19104
215/662-5606
Responsible for: Delaware, District of Columbia, Maryland, New Jersey, New York, Pennsylvania, Puerto Rico, Virgin Islands

New England Association of Schools and Colleges
209 Burlington Road
Bedford, MA 01730-1433
617/271-0022
Responsible for: Connecticut, Maine, Massachusetts, New Hampshire, Rhode Island, Vermont

North Central Association of Colleges and Schools
159 N. Dearborn Street
Chicago, IL 60601
800/621-7440
Responsible for: Arizona, Arkansas, Colorado, Illinois, Indiana, Iowa, Kansas, Michigan, Minnesota, Missouri, Nebraska, New Mexico, North Dakota, Ohio, Oklahoma, South Dakota, West Virginia, Wisconsin, Wyoming

Northwest Association of Schools and Colleges
3700 University Way N.E.
Seattle, WA 98105
206/543-0195
Responsible for: Alaska, Idaho, Montana, Nevada, Oregon, Utah, Washington

Southern Association of Colleges and Schools
1866 Southern Lane
Decatur, GA 30033-4097
404/679-4500

Responsible for: Alabama, Florida, Georgia, Kentucky, Louisiana, Mississippi, North Carolina, South Carolina, Tennessee, Texas, Virginia

Western Association of Schools and Colleges
Box 9990, Mills College
Oakland, CA 94613
510/632-5000
Responsible for: California, Hawaii, Guam, Trust Territory of the Pacific

Getting Started

    The first thing to do is send for the catalogue and admission forms for the schools you're interested in. There is normally an application fee of $25-$50 for each school. Mail in your application, along with other required items such as transcripts and letters of recommendation. It is advisable to start the application process up to a year in advance of the anticipated start of study; it takes from four to six months to receive a reply. Unlike regular on-campus attendance, many distance study programs do not require any entrance examinations.

Types of Courses You Can Take Through Distance Study

Correspondence Courses

    Correspondence courses, as the name implies, are primarily conducted in written form through the mail or by fax. Generally, enrollment can take place at any time of the year with a six to twelve month time limit for completing the course. Many schools now have toll-free telephone numbers for students to contact instructors to ask questions and receive guidance. The student receives a course syllabus that outlines the scope of study and gives detailed study guidelines. Supplementary materials include texts of lectures and excerpts from articles, along with the instructor's comments. Some schools provide textbooks as part of the cost of the course; more often the student orders them from the university's bookstore. A course consists of up to twenty separate lessons, and usually requires written assignments, a term paper, a test the student takes and sends in to be graded by the instructor, and a final exam. Final exams normally must be monitored by a proctor, an individual holding some kind of academic position selected by the student and approved by the school administering the course by means of an application process.

Independent Guided Study—the Learning Contract

Increasingly, schools are offering independent study programs where the student and a faculty advisor design a course of study for the student to carry out independently. Many of these programs use a Learning Contract, an organized plan that the student and faculty advisor agree upon that outlines specific objectives, describes the scope of study, and designates methods and resources to be used to complete a certain part of the student's degree plan. A Learning Contract may include typical college subject areas, or be composed of an innovative program of nontraditional study designed by the student. This plan is carried out independently with faculty guidance via phone, mail, computer, or fax. This is the most flexible method of home study, requiring no fixed time schedules and a very wide range of topics. Students are encouraged to use the resources of their local college and public libraries.

Courses Offered by Cable or Satellite

Some schools broadcast courses over cable television in local areas. Also, some colleges offer live classes locally through interactive video teleconferencing at designated sites. A nationwide consortium of ten universities offers courses via national cable television through Mind Extension University.

Video Courses Offered at Corporate Sites

Professional courses of study may be available through video at corporate sites. An on-site facilitator is usually present to offer guidance, answer questions, and administer exams.

Courses Offered Through Interactive Computer

For courses offered by computer, home computers can be linked with the university computer by means of a modem. Students meet with professors and participate in class discussions asynchronously, at their own convenience (within a time frame of about a week for classes).

Noncredit Courses

Many schools allow students to enroll in credit courses on a noncredit basis for personal satisfaction.

Getting Academic Credit For Things You Already Know

You may be surprised to discover that you can earn college credit for things you've already done; for knowledge gained in life and work experience that is relevant to your degree program. The kinds of life experience that may be turned into credit are those that offer learning that is equivalent to what is gained in a college course. Don't be intimidated by this, however. Many things you've already learned most likely will fall into this category. For example, playing your favorite sport may be very similar to taking a college class in physical education. If you know how to play a musical instrument, your knowledge may be comparable to that gained in college instruction. The many varied tasks of homemaking encompass academic fields such as business (planning and budgeting), psychology (interpersonal communication among family members), education (child raising), and nutrition (meal planning and cooking). If English is your second language, you can probably receive enough credit for the proficiency you have in your native language to fulfill an undergraduate program's language requirement. Travel or living abroad offers significant knowledge in cross-cultural communication, art, history, geography, and more. Things you may have watched on TV, such as a public television series, are creditworthy educational experiences, as well as talking to or listening to knowledgeable people in all kinds of fields. And then there's your own reading and research on topics of special interest to you.

How Does Life Experience Get Turned into Academic Credit?
The experience has to be documented, usually by means of a written description in a formal presentation called a portfolio. This is evaluated by faculty members who then assign credit. For each documented life experience activity you have to show that learning took place in areas of academic significance. For example, if you have been a small business owner and want to get credit for it, you might want to show that this experience gave you knowledge and expertise in the areas of management, personnel, finance, marketing, advertising, and business planning. You have to translate the activity you're documenting into academic terms. Although each school has its own standards for judging the quality of the portfolio presentation and awarding credit, many issue guidelines to students and offer courses that assist in the preparation of portfolios.

For information about publications that give assistance in

preparing portfolios, contact the Council for Adult and Experiential Learning (223 West Jackson Boulevard, #510, Chicago, IL 60606; 312/ 922-5909). One of the Council's guidebooks contains sample portfolio information (Lois Lamdin, Earned College Credit for What You Know; $26.50).

There are no universally accepted standards for what kinds of life experience are worthy of academic credit, but progress is being made in this direction. The American Council on Education, a private organization, publishes guidelines, and schools are beginning to agree on the amount of credit to award for many types of activities. Here are some of the activities for which credit has been granted:

recitals
performances
honors and awards
speeches
articles
arts and crafts
writing samples
slides and videotapes
recommendations
interviews
job descriptions
designs, blueprints
works of art
films, photographs

There are many non-collegiate seminars and workshops, training programs, and formal courses sponsored by business, industry, government, the military, and private associations for which credit is awarded. The American Council of Education gives specific recommendations for the amount of credit to be granted for many of these programs in its reference work, The National Guide to Educational Credit for Training Programs. Some of the types of courses you can get academic credit for:

machine technician
equipment operator
sales and marketing
corporate management training
telecommunications
inspirational—achieving one's potential
typing/keyboarding
publishing

9

electronics
mediation/negotiation
teletype
postal service
business
consumer credit
real estate
insurance
banking
automotive
leadership
marketing
industrial training
police, fire service
motivational courses
personnel
weather forecasting
paralegal
computer
emergency medical technician
health and safety programs
music
sports (example: sailing)
secretarial
executive training programs
vocational-technical
government and military
language courses
pilot, air traffic control
seamanship
ministerial—seminary
health service
interpersonal skills
child care
agriculture

There's a growing trend for colleges and universities to recognize life experiences as a valid way of attaining college-level learning, so you might get credit for things you never imagined. Here are some more ideas, for inspiration, of activities that might be considered worthy of college credit:

jury duty

apprenticeship training
informal teaching (church, recreation)
using statistics in sports or gambling
giving a talk or presentation to a club meeting
leading a Scout troop
being a dedicated filmgoer
attending concerts and lectures
participating in a Great Books class
gardening
designing clothes and sewing
running for a local office
writing news releases
studying and looking for antiques
building a house or cabin
traveling
going to museums
studying emergency medicine
planning and building a playground
attending meetings and seminars
playing an instrument in a local orchestra
learning new philosophies and religions
taking a dance class
riding and grooming horses
being an amateur photographer and developing film
being active in local politics
teaching children crafts
weaving fabric
acting in a play
sailing and navigating
volunteering with senior citizens
doing your own car repairs
building furniture
raising and training animals
quilting
making pottery
painting a portrait
building sets for a community theater
negotiating a deal
living in a different culture
helping with a small business
body-building and researching nutrition

reading poetry and literature
reading magazines
visiting historical sites
helping a disabled person
being active in the P.T.A.
writing for a newspaper
cooking an international dinner
studying alternative medicine

Credit May Be Earned for What You Already Know (Or are Willing to Learn On Your Own) By Taking Equivalency Examinations

Most schools award credit toward undergraduate degrees by means of equivalency examinations, but very few allow most or all of the required credit for a degree to be earned by means of exams. A few graduate degree programs accept credit on the basis of exams. Many schools have their own exams, which are similar to course final exams and give credit equivalent to a college course in the subject. There are also two national agencies that provide standardized exams; these are used by most schools. The College-Level Examination Program (CLEP) is administered by the Educational Testing Service (CLEP, P.O. Box 6600, Princeton, New Jersey 08541-6600). The Proficiency Examination Program (PEP) is offered by the American College Testing Program (P.O. Box 4014, Iowa City, IA 52243) and in New York by Regents External Degree—College Proficiency Programs (Cultural Education Center, Albany, NY 12230). These tests are adminstered at colleges and universities at the convenience of the school and the degree candidate. CLEP exams are offered in these general subject areas: Social Science and History, English Composition, Humanities, Mathematics, and Natural Science. Individual exams are available in these fields:

American Government
American History I and II
Educational Psychology
General Psychology
Human Growth and Development
Principles of Marketing
Introductory Macroeconomics
Introductory Sociology
Western Civilization I and II
French I and II

German I and II
Spanish I and II
American Literature
College Composition
Analysis and Interpretation
English Literature
Freshman English
Trigonometry
Algebra and Trigonometry
General Biology
General Chemistry
Information Systems and Computer Applications
Introduction to Management
Introductory Accounting
Introductory Business Law
Calculus and Elementary Functions
College Algebra
English Composition with Essay (given four times a year)

PEP exams are available in the following subject areas: Arts and Sciences, Business, Education, and Nursing. Specific exams subjects include:
Abnormal Psychology
Anatomy and Physiology
Foundations of Gerontology
Microbiology
Physical Geology
Statistics
Business Policy
Corporation Finance
Introductory Accounting
Organizational Behavior
Principles of Management
Principles of Marketing
Production/Operations Management
Educational Psychology
Reading Instruction in the Elementary School
Reading Instruction: Theoretical Foundations
Fundamentals of Nursing
Maternal and Child Nursing
Psychiatric/Mental Health Nursing (plus 14 more nursing ex-

aminations)

Most of the tests offered by CLEP are available in multiple-choice format with or without an accompanying essay question section. All of the exams are ninety minutes long and cost around $40 each. The PEP tests are up to three hours long and cost from $40 to $125 each exam.

The testing organizations offer detailed syllabi outlining the content of each test. The testing agencies now make copies of the tests available to the public. In addition, there are many good books available on preparing for these exams; some provide complete sample tests. Check out your local library's reference section or a good bookstore. Many local individuals (graduate students and professors) and groups offer assistance in studying for these exams. In addition, the Stanley H. Kaplan Educational Centers, located in most states, offer classes and rental materials for home study (131 West 56th Street, New York, NY 10019; 212/977-8200 or toll free 800-223-1782).

Other Examinations:

Examinations used by the University of the State of New York's Regents College are made available nationally by the American College Testing Proficiency Examination Program. These examinations, which are used by colleges and universities nationwide to award course credits, have been recommended by the American Council on Education.

Some schools award credit for successful performance on the Graduate Record Examination (GRE/ETS, P.O. Box 6000, Princeton, New Jersey 08541-6600; 609-771-7670). There are advanced exams that measure bachelor's degree level knowledge in many fields: biology, chemistry, computer science, economics, education, engineering, French, geography, geology, German, history, English literature, mathematics, music, philosophy, physics, political science, psychology, sociology, and Spanish.

The Defense Activity for Non-Traditional Educational Support (DANTES) is a testing program for military personnel; contact your military education officer for more information.

TRANSFER CREDIT

Most distance-education programs recognize transfer credit from another accredited institution. Some schools have an affiliation with one or more universities whereby transfer credit is automatically accepted. Students wishing to have credit from foreign academic institutions transferred may have these educational credentials evaluated by one of the private organizations that provide this service, usually at a cost of between $60 and $150. Some of these services evaluate non-academic experiential learning as well. Many schools rely on the recommendations of such services; others evaluate the foreign credentials of their applicants themselves. Here are some of the organizations that provide evaluation services for students with foreign credentials:

Credentials Evaluation Service
P.O. Box 24040
Los Angeles, CA 90024
310/390-6276

Educational Credential Evaluators, Inc.
P.O. Box 92970
Milwaukee, WI 53203-0970
414/289-3400

International Consultants of Delaware, Inc.
109 Barksdale Professional Center
Newark, DE 19711
302/737-8715

International Education Research Foundation
P.O. Box 66940
Los Angeles, CA 90066
310/390-6276

World Education Services
P.O. Box 745
Old Chelsea Station
New York, NY 10113
212/966-6311

THE REGENTS CREDIT BANK

The Department of Education of the state of New York operates the Regents Credit Bank, which is a service available to anyone that evaluates and consolidates academic credits from many sources into a single transcript that is widely accepted.

Here are the types of data that can be recorded on a Regents

Credit Bank transcript:

> 1) credit from resident college courses, correspondence courses, or independent study;
> 2) scores on equivalency tests (including military);
> 3) extrainstitutional learning experiences such as workshops, seminars, and corporate training programs that have been approved by the American Council on Education or the New York National Program on Noncollegiate Sponsored Instruc tion;
> 4) Federal Aviation Administration certificates and pilot licenses;
> 5) nursing credentials from approved examinations.

A special assessment procedure is available for the evaluation of life experiences for credit. The student meets with a panel of experts in Albany, New York. They may require written documents or articles, works of art, or performances as appropriate to determine the amount of credit to be given. A credit bank account costs around $250, which includes the in-house evaluation. Negative information may be omitted from the transcript. (Regents Credit Bank, Regents College, University of the State of New York, 7 Columbia Circle, Albany, NY 12203-5159).

Part 2
Program Profiles

ACADIA UNIVERSITY

Contact:
Acadia University
Wolfville, Nova Scotia
Canada BOP 1X0
(902) 542-2201 Ext. 1434

Telephone:
800-565-6568
FAX: (902) 542-3715
Electronic Switchboard: (902) 542-2200 Ext. 1434

Degrees Offered:
Certificate and Diploma in Business Administration, Certificate in Computer Science.

Summary: Correspondence courses by mail in a wide variety of subjects in business and the humanities. Students have six to twelve months to complete courses. Off-campus exams must be written at another university or college.

Fees:
Application fee: $25
3 credit-hour course: $307
6 credit-hour course: $615
International students:
3 credit-hour course: $632
6 credit-hour course: $1265
Final examination fee for an off-campus exam: $45.
Other fees may apply

Residency: none

Narration:
Acadia University was founded in 1838 by the Baptist denomination. At a time when other similar universities had sectarian requirements for students and teachers, Acadia was founded in response to a need to provide educational opportunities to students regardless of religious denomination.

Acadia offers correspondence courses that may be taken from anywhere in the world that has access to mail service. Courses are offered in a wide variety of subjects in business and the humanities. Some courses make extensive use of audio and/ or video cassettes. A Biology by Video program is available with some courses requiring on-campus laboratory work.

The maximum length of time allotted to finish a correspondence course is 6 months for a 3 credit-hour course and 12 months for a 6 credit-hour course. Students must be registered in a correspondence course for a minimum of 3 months to be eligible to write the final examination. Correspondence final exams are written during regularly scheduled university exam periods. Off-campus exams are available, to be written at another university or college.

Textbooks may be ordered by mail or phone. Upon completion of a course the bookstore buys back books that are still current.

ADAM SMITH UNIVERSITY

Contact:
Adam Smith University
3350 Ridgelake Drive
Suite 200
Metarie, Louisiana 70002

Telephone:
800-732-3796

Degrees Offered: Associate, Bachelor's, and Master's—major programs in business, liberal arts and sciences, nursing, chiropractic, medical and health technology, computer science and veterinary technology.

Summary: Degree programs for adults in career areas and liberal arts; admission policies are flexible and personalized; a student may enroll at any time.

19

Fees:

Application/evaluation fee: $50
Transfer credit fee for Associate Degree: $1250
Transfer credit fee for Bachelor's Degree: $2500
Transfer credit fee for Master's Degree: $1500
Undergraduate credit: $150 per credit
Graduate credit: $175 per credit

Accreditation:

Currently licensed by the Board of Regents of the State of Louisiana. Licensed institutions have met minimal operational standards set forth by the state, but licensure does not constitute accreditation, guarantee the transferability of credit, or signify that programs are certifiable by any professional agency or organization.

Residency: none

Narration:

Adam Smith University was founded in 1991 to offer degree programs at the Associate, Bachelor's, and Master's degree levels for students who want an alternative to traditional university degree programs. There are opportunities for students to package prior learning at other institutions to achieve a degree. Some students receive their degrees from Adam Smith University through transferring academic work from one or more other institutions of higher learning. Others combine work from colleges and universities with credit from non- traditional sources such as proficiency examinations, experience in a variety of careers and professions, other relevant life and work experience and independent study to receive their degree. Adam Smith University accepts course work completed at other recognized institutions no matter when the course was taken, and does not limit the amount of credit transferred from other institutions. Courses sponsored by trade associations, by business and industry and by the military are acceptable for credit towards degrees at Adam Smith University. Students are encouraged to plan individual university degree programs and to design a major area of concentration that fits individual career and personal goals.

A student may enroll at any time. Graduation takes place whenever all degree requirements are completed.

AMERICAN COLLEGE

Contact:
The American College
270 S. Bryn Mawr Avenue
Bryn Mawr, Pennsylvania 19010

mailing address:
The American College
P.O. Box 1513
Bryn Mawr, Pennsylvania 19010-1513

Telephone:
215-526-1490
FAX: 215-526-1465

Degrees Offered: Master of Science in Financial Services (M.S.F.S.), Master of Science in Management (M.S.M.); professional courses: Chartered Life Underwriter, Chartered Financial Consultant

Summary: Master's degree programs for financial services professionals combining distance learning with limited on-campus study

Fees:
Admission/Application fee: $275
Tuition (per course): $475
Residency tuition (each one-week session): $1,300

Accreditation: Middle States Association of Colleges and Schools

Residency: Limited; two one-week sessions

Narration:
The American College offers professional certification and graduate degree education to men and women seeking career growth in the financial services marketplace. Courses are developed by a resident faculty and taken by thousands of students across the nation and abroad who study independently or in local classes. Final examinations are administered at local test centers.
The Master of Science in Financial Services, designed for

financial services professionals, emphasizes problem solving, analytical and communications skills in coursework, and an independent research/writing project. Each distance course concludes with a computerized, objective examination that students can take at their convenience in a nationwide network of test centers. Flexible scheduling, with course load determined according to individual preferences, permits students to set their own pace in planning their program. Two one-week residency sessions are required on campus.

The Master of Science in Management degree program is a sequence of courses designed to provide maximum study flexibility for the student through self-study and two one-week residency programs on campus. Each course is constructed to blend theory and application to increase the effectiveness of managers in field services. The curriculum provides education for professionals that is focused on managerial leadership, integrating the components of leadership and management into the educational experience.

The Chartered Life Underwriter is a 10-course program for insurance agents, field managers, and home office personnel. The Chartered Financial Consultant is a 10-course program for financial consultants and others in financial services.

THE AMERICAN UNIVERSITY IN LONDON

Contact:
The Registrar
The American University in London
Archway Central Hall
Archway Close
London N19 3TD
United Kingdom

Telephone: 071-263-2986
International: 010-44-71-263-2986
Telex: 081-895-1182 GECOMS G
International: 010-44-81-895-1182 GEOCOMS G

FAX: 071-281-2815
International: 010-44-71-281-2815

Degrees Offered: Bachelor's, Master's and Ph.D.

Summary: Flexible, non-traditional degree programs that accept credits earned by a variety of means; non-residents study independently under the direction of an Academic Supervisor.

Fees: (approximate, depending on the current exchange rate)
Registration fee: $37
For non-resident students tuition is charged for the whole year
All certificate courses (English, Business Studies, Computer Science) $1425
All degree and diploma courses: $4763
Non-degree courses (per semester credit hour) $180
Examination fee: $112
Graduation fee: $112
Laboratory fee: (if applicable) $825
Library fee: $90

Residency: none

Narration:

The American University in London, incorporated in the United States, is a non-profit corporation organized to promote and provide education in scientific and non-scientific fields. The Distance Learning Center offers non-traditional programs of supervised study and research leading to Bachelor's, Master's and Ph.D. degree programs in liberal arts, business administration, education, engineering, law, pharmacy and natural sciences. Study and research can be carried out by a student living away from the University under the supervision of an approved Academic Supervisor. The heart of this innovative educational program is the opportunity to earn credits for a degree by a variety of means, including independent study and research, published work, nationally approved examinations, and courses offered by the armed forces.

ANTIOCH UNIVERSITY

Contact:
Antioch University School for Adult and Experiential Learning
Office of Admissions
800 Livermore Street
Yellow Springs, Ohio 45387

Telephone:
513-767-6325

Degrees Offered: Individualized Master of Arts Degree (M.A.), Master of Arts in Conflict Resolution (M.A.)

Summary: Graduate programs for non-resident national and international students with diverse program designs.

Fees:
Tuition per quarter: $1275
Other fees may apply

Accreditation: North Central Association of Colleges and Schools

Residency: limited

Narration:
Antioch University was founded in 1852 in Yellow Springs, Ohio as a private, liberal arts college. Horace Mann, known as the architect of the American public school system, became its first president and guided the institution's development with his philosophy of educating the "whole person."

Antioch University School for Adult and Experiential Learning was founded in 1988 to offer an undergraduate Antioch education to adult students within commuting distance, and to guide and develop graduate programs serving Ohio as well as graphically dispersed national and international populations through its diverse program designs.

The Individualized Master of Arts Degree offers students an opportunity to participate in the design of their master's programs and to complete the work in their own communities. It is a limited residency program designed for academically excellent students

24

who are motivated to manage their own educational plans. Individual learning components may be tailored to the student's educational goals and preferred learning style. A student's degree plan may include courses taught at another university, practica, workshops, mentorships, and independent study. Students must come to the Yellow Springs campus twice during the program: for a 5-day orientation seminar and for a 4-day thesis seminar. The average amount of time required for completion of the program is two to two-and-one-half years.

ATHABASCA UNIVERSITY

Contact:
Athabasca University Learning Centre
Second Floor, North Tower
Seventh Street Plaza
10030-107 Street Edmonton, AB
Canada T5J 3E4

Telephone:
403-675-6168
Exam Requests: 403-675-6386
FAX: 403-675-6174

Degrees Offered:
Bachelor of Administration, Bachelor of Arts, Bachelor of Commerce, Bachelor of General Studies, Bachelor of Nursing, Bachelor of Science. University certificates are available in a variety of fields.

Summary: Correspondence courses and degree programs for Canadians living anywhere. Exams must be taken at an acceptable university location.

Fees:
Application fee: $40
Materials handling fee: $70
Evaluation fee: $45
tuition:
3 credits (Canadian) $300.00

25

6 credits (Canadian) $530.00
3 credits - Foreign (Grandfathered) $415.00
6 credits - Foreign (Grandfathered) $760.00
3 credits - Foreign (Non-Grandfathered) $530.00
6 Credits - Foreign (Non-Grandfathered) $990.00

Accreditation: Full member of the Association of Universities and Colleges of Canada, the Association of Commonwealth Universities, the International Council for Distance Education, and the Canadian Association for Distance Education

Residency: Students must be Canadian citizens/permanent residents, but those who are temporarily residing outside Canada may be admitted, provided they have a permanent address within Canada.

Narration:

Athabasca University makes it possible for people to earn a university education regardless of where they live or work, or their commitments to careers or families. Open education achieves this flexibility by using a variety of methods to deliver courses: print, telephone, radio, television, laboratories, workshops, computer-assisted learning, audio- and video-cassettes, classroom, and seminar sessions. Reading courses are offered that are based almost entirely on assigned texts. Courses are offered in four major fields of study—applied studies, humanities, science, and social sciences.

The central component of most courses is the home-study learning package. Each package is a learning system that may include textbooks, workbooks, audio- and video-cassettes, project kits, study guides, manuals, and computer disks. Six months' completion time is allowed for a three or four credit course, and 12 months for a six credit course. Telephone tutors are available for most home-study courses. Seminar classes are held through teleconference methods, and radio and television programs form an integral part of some courses. For students living at a distance from the University, exams are monitored by an acceptable volunteer provided by the student.

ATLANTIC UNION COLLEGE

Contact:
Adult Degree Program
Atlantic Union College
P.O. Box 1000
South Lancaster, Massachusetts 01561

Telephone:
508-368-2300
toll free: 800-282-2030
FAX: 508-368-2015

Degrees Offered:
Bachelor of Arts (B.A.), Bachelor of Music (B.M.), Bachelor of Science (B.S.), Master of Education (M.Ed.)

Summary: Seventh-day Adventist college that accepts all students interested in education based on Christian and liberal arts principles. Students organize their own units of study involving their work, creative experiences, travel, or research.

Fees
Tuition per unit of study: $2,950
Fees per unit of study: $40
Challenge Exam Fee ($50 per test plus 1/2 tuition)
Other fees may apply

Accreditation: New England Association of Schools and Colleges

Residency: limited; attendance required at eight- or ten-day seminar at the beginning of each unit of study (twice a year)

Narration:
The Adult Degree Program at Atlantic Union College is based on the belief that many adults whose college work has been interrupted by marriage, work, military service, or other personal circumstances, should have the opportunity of completing their degrees, and that there are many ways of doing valid academic work other than being enrolled in on-campus courses. Founded in 1882 by the Seventh-day Adventist Church, the college now

educates students for many professions and occupations in the church, community, and the larger society. The campus welcomes qualified students who are interested in an education structured on Christian and liberal arts principles.

Students come to the Adult Degree Program campus for a mandatory eight- or ten-day seminar in January or July at the beginning of each unit of study. When students enter the program, a committee evaluates their past academic experience and determines the number of units required to complete a degree. The possibilities within a unit are open and flexible in most cases. Study units may involve reading and research, practical on-the-job experience, or creative work. Some students combine travel and study. The fact that they are not limited to courses being offered allows students to explore areas of academic significance that they would not be able to study in a more conventional program. Students work at home under the direction of study supervisors that they communicate with by mail, tape recording, phone, computer network, or personal conferences where possible.

BASTYR COLLEGE

Contact:
Bastyr College
Natural Health Sciences
Continuing Education Department
144 N.E. 54th
Seattle, Washington 98105

Telephone:
206-523-9585
FAX: 206-527-4763

Degrees Offered: No degree programs are offered through Distance Learning. All courses may be applied to a B.S. Degree in Natural Health Sciences with a major in Nutrition.

Summary: Courses in natural health and nutrition

Fees:
$125 per credit; $375 per 3-hour course
Course materials average $50 per course

Accreditation: Northwest Association of Schools and Colleges

Residency: none

Narration:

The Distance Learning program was established to meet the educational needs of people interested in learning more about natural health and nutrition but who are unable to become full-time, resident students. The distance learning concept involves regular written and spoken dialogue between the student and instructor through written assignments and a toll-free telephone number.

The student receives textbooks and a course study guide which outlines specific assignments required for the course and provides information about the faculty member assigned to the student. Learning materials for some courses may also include audio cassettes and/or video tapes. Course work is completed in a period of time between eight and sixteen weeks.

The courses available through Distance Learning are: Nutrition I and II; Nutrition and Herbs; Nutrition and the Natural Products Industry; Introduction to Nutrition in Natural Medicine, Diet and Behavior; and Fundamental Principles of Chinese Medicine.

BEMIDJI STATE UNIVERSITY

Contact:
Bemidji State University
Center for Extended Learning
Attn: External Studies Program
Deputy Hall Box 27
1500 Birchmont Drive NE
Bemidji, Minnesota 56601-2699

Telephone:
218/755-3924
Toll free: 800-475-2001 ext. 3924 or 2738

Degrees Offered: Associate of Arts (A.A.), Associate of Science in Criminal Justice (A.S.),   Bachelor of Science (B.S.), Bachelor of Arts (B.A.) in Criminal Justice, Social Studies and History

Summary: Undergraduate courses in liberal arts and criminal justice offered by correspondence

Fees: Available upon request

Accreditation: North Central Association of Colleges and Schools

Residency: None for correspondence courses. For degree programs, 45 out of 192 credits must be earned in residence.

Narration:

External Studies courses are offered at the undergraduate level only. Students may register for classes four times a year; August, November, February and June. Home study is facilitated by a syllabus, supplements, audio cassettes and video cassettes, which are mailed. Students have a twelve-week block of time in which to complete a class. Exams may be taken in the student's home town with a designated test administrator.

BEREAN COLLEGE OF THE ASSEMBLIES OF GOD

Contact:
Berean College
1445 Boonville Avenue
Springfield, Missouri 65802

Telephone:
417/862-2781, ext. 2313
FAX: 417/862-2781, ext. 1222

Degrees Offered: Associate of Arts (A.A.) degree in Bible/Theology, Church Ministries, or Ministerial Studies. Bachelor of Arts (B.A.) in Bible/Theology, Pastoral Ministries, Christian Education, or Christian Counseling

Summary: Correspondence courses in Christian education with many flexible options for obtaining credit for life experiences

Fees:
Credit-for-Life-Experience Evaluation: $40
Credit for Life Experience Tuition (per credit): $10
Tuition (per credit): $69
Credit by Exam Fee (per course): $40
Examination Re-take Fee: $25

Accreditation: National Home Study Council

Residency: none

Narration:

Berean College, an integral part of the Assemblies of God church, embraces Bible-based objectives. Correspondence courses are only one of many options available for distance education. Students may receive credit for courses simply by taking the final examination. Credit for life experiences is granted for skills and knowledge gained outside the classroom. Some of the life experiences which are now being recognized as legitimate learning activities are on-the-job learning, non-credit postsecondary programs, significant volunteer social work, executive leadership, and other experiences that parallel academic study programs, as well as general knowledge gained through life experience. If a student's knowledge in a specific subject area is similar to that described in the catalog for a Berean College course, and that learning can be documented, the student may submit a Petition for College Credit. Through this process, a student may earn up to 25% of the credits required for a B.A. degree.

The time limit for completing a course from the time of enrollment is 12 months. The college encourages contact between faculty and student at least once every 30 days. Final exams must be taken in the presence of a proctor who meets the requirements of the college.

BRIGHAM YOUNG UNIVERSITY

Contact:
Brigham Young University
Degrees by Independent Study
315 Harman Building
Brigham Young University
Provo, Utah 84602-1515

Telephone:
801-378-4351

Degrees Offered: Bachelor of Independent Studies

Summary: Mormon university that offers liberal arts education with emphasis in the humanities; major study areas include Man and the Meaning of Life, Man and Society, Man and Beauty, and Man and the Universe

Fees:
Foundations class (8 semester hours): $495
Tuition (per semester hour) $62 up to 12 hours; more than 12 hours $745.

Accreditation: Northwest Association of Colleges and Schools

Residency: limited

Narration:
Brigham Young University was founded in 1875 and is now the largest church-sponsored university in the United States. The student progresses through designated phases of study. The Preparation Phase includes courses such as How to Think and How to Communicate. The Growth Phase course offerings include Philosophy, World Religions, Family, Race Relations, Theater, Music, and various classes in mathematics and the sciences.

Once enrolled in a study area, students are expected to complete at least one assignment every six months. Students have two years from the date of enrollment in a study area to complete it and up to eight years to complete the degree. Students write to, talk with, or send a cassette tape to the instructor at least once a month during the time they are doing course work. Graduation requirements include some two-week, full-time seminars that are mandatory. However, some seminars may be waived if the student has sufficient transfer credits.

CALIFORNIA STATE UNIVERSITY, DOMINGUEZ HILLS

Contact:
California State University
Dominguez Hills
Humanities External Degree Program, SAC 2/2126
1000 East Victoria St.
Carson, California 90747

Telephone:
310-516-3743
310-516-4028
FAX: 310-516-3971 - Extended Education
        310-516-3449 - Campus Mailroom
Internet: huxonline @dhvx20.csudh.edu

Degrees Offered: Master of Arts (M.A.) in Humanities

Summary: M.A. degree offered through independent study correspondence courses with an individualized approach.

Accreditation: Western Association of Schools and Colleges

Residency: none

Narration:
        California State University now consists of 20 campuses across the state with over 350,000 full-time and part-time students and a faculty of more than 18,000. The Dominguez Hills campus is one of the fastest growing branches of this university.
        The Master of Arts in the Humanities offers a broad inter-

disciplinary exposure to all of the areas of the Humanities—history, literature, philosophy, music, and art—and the establishment of an integrated perspective among them with emphasis on their interrelating effects and influences. The student is provided with the opportunity to specialize in a particular discipline of the Humanities, or in specific cultural thematic areas which may be traced across all of the humanistic disciplines.

The Humanities stress major areas: cultural knowledge, perceptual skills, and creative production. Each course is accompanied with a student study guide—a specially prepared packet, produced by the faculty, to provide the framework for independent learning. The guides may include such material as cassette tapes, art reproductions, excerpts from important writers and their works, study questions, explanations of terms and concepts, bibliographical essays, and short monographs.

Students are now given the option of taking selected courses by computer via the international Internet network. This is an alternative mode of delivery to the current curriculum delivery system. Students with access to a personal computer and modem or other telecommunications linking device may use the system to contact instructors, send assignments, receive course guides and materials, converse with fellow students, and do online research.

CALDWELL COLLEGE

Contact:
Caldwell College
External Degree Program
9 Ryerson Avenue
Caldwell, New Jersey 07006

Telephone:
201-228-4424, ext. 215
FAX: 201-228-3851

Degrees Offered: Bachelor of Arts (B.A.), Bachelor of Fine Arts (B.F.A.), Bachelor of Science (B.S.)

Summary: Catholic four-year liberal arts institution committed to intellectual rigor, individual attention, and the ethical values of the Judeo-Christian academic tradition

Fees:
Application fee: $25
Tuition per credit: $220

Accreditation: Middle States Association of Colleges and Schools

Residency: Limited—each semester begins with a required weekend orientation program with workshops designed to enhance the student's college experience. Additionally, some on-campus course work is required for degrees in art and computer information systems.

Narration:
The External Degree Program offers adults age 23 and older an opportunity to earn a college degree without attending classes on campus. Through guided independent study, adults in this program complete the same challenging assignments as on-campus students. Through the semester students learn through tutorial study augmented by interaction with the faculty via phone and personal conferences, mail-in assignments, audio, video and computer technologies. Students may enroll in one to five courses during a semester depending on their personal schedule and ability. The program offers three semesters: fall, spring, and summer.

CALIFORNIA COLLEGE FOR HEALTH SCIENCES

Contact:
California College for Health Sciences
222 West 24th Street
National City, California 91950

Telephone:
619-477-4800

35

Degrees Offered: Associate of Science (A.S.) with an Emphasis in Allied Health, Bachelor of Science (B.S.) with an Emphasis in Health Services Management, Master of Science (M.S.) with an Emphasis in Community Health Administration and Wellness Promotion

Summary: Health-related degree programs that are free of classroom, seminar and on-campus requirements; students work at their own pace

Fees:
Per 3-credit lower division course: $235
Per 3-credit upper division course: $335
Per 3-credit graduate level course: $335
(Tuition covers all instructional materials, testing and student services)

Accreditation: National Home Study Council

Residency: none

Narration:
Specifically designed to meet the needs of working adults, the College offers external degree programs completed entirely through independent study. These programs are free of classroom, seminar and on-campus requirements. Students set their own pace, and may enroll in one or more courses at a time.

The Associate of Science degree is offered to allied health professionals who have previously earned the equivalent of 30 lower division semester credits in an allied health specialty. These credits can come from a combination of college credits and prior experiential learning. Also offered are associate degree studies in respiratory care, medical transcription, EEG and early childhood education.

The Bachelor of Science program is a "hands-on" degree preparing allied health professionals to meet new demands and challenges that come with management positions. Sixty lower division credits are required for admission.

The Master of Science degree program is designed for professionals whose career responsibilities have expanded into administration and programming of health care systems. A

36

bachelor's degree earned from an accredited institution is required for admission to the program. The curriculum emphasizes business management, human resource program development and counseling skills.

CALIFORNIA COAST UNIVERSITY

Contact:
California Coast University
700 N. Main Street
P.O. Box 11745
Santa Ana, California 92711-9898

Telephone:
714-547-9625

Degrees Offered: Bachelor of Science (B.S.) in Business Administration, Management, Psychology; Master of Business Administration (M.B.A.); Master of Science (M.S.) in Engineering, Psychology; Doctor of Philosophy (Ph.D.) in Business Administration, Management, Engineering, Psychology; Doctor of Education (Ed.D.)

Summary: Non-traditional, self-paced undergraduate and graduate degree programs. Students may take exams to demonstrate proficiency in a course area and receive credit for non-college experiential learning.

Fees: (non U.S.-resident fees are slightly higher)
(per semester)
Bachelor's degree programs: $2475
Master's degree programs: $2575
Ph.D. programs: $3075
Concurrent Bachelor's/Master's Degree Programs: $2975
Concurrent Master's/Doctoral Degree Programs: $3475

Accreditation: Council for Private Postsecondary and Vocational Education

Residency: none

Narration:

The University provides an alternative method of education utilizing a nontraditional approach to meeting the needs of mature men and women from all areas of industry, business, education and the helping professions.

Students may complete all course work, reading, research and writing requirements through prescriptive independent study programs under faculty guidance and supervision. All programs are self-paced, providing students an opportunity to advance as rapidly or as slowly as his/her time and ability permit.

After a student is enrolled, all non-college experience is reviewed to determine if the individual has adequate experience to take a Challenge Examination to demonstrate an acceptable level of competence in each specific course required in the degree program. On the undergraduate level, students may request Credit by Experiential Learning for general elective courses and major courses. Where an adequate level of competence is identified, Study Guides referenced to specific textbooks are provided and completed under faculty and staff guidance.

All students will select a topic for research, which may be related to occupation or work experience if appropriate for the student's major in the program.

The opportunity is available to pursue concurrent Bachelor's/Master's Degree programs and Concurrent Master's/Doctoral Degree programs.

CENTRAL MICHIGAN UNIVERSITY

Contact:
Extended Degree Programs
Central Michigan University
Attn: Office of the Executive Director
Rowe Hall 131
Mt. Pleasant, Michigan 48859

Telephone:
800-950-1144, ext. 3868

Degrees Offered: Bachelor of Science (B.S.) in Community Development or Administration (available in Michigan only); Master of Science (M.S.) in Administration; Master of Arts (M.A.) in Humanities; Master of Education (M.Ed.; offered in group format only)

Summary: Telecourses, correspondence courses, learning packages, and prior learning credit provide flexible means for earning a bachelor's or master's degree.

Fees:
Application Fee: $40
Correspondence Courses (per semester hour): $115
Learning Packages (per semester hour)
    Undergraduate: $115
Extended Credit Courses (per semester hour)
    Undergraduate: $115
    Graduate: $126
Prior Learning Portfolio: $65
Prior Learning Assessment Recording Fee: $25

Accreditation: North Central Association of Colleges and Schools; National Council for Accreditation of Teacher Education

Residency: none

Narration:
    A major goal of Central Michigan University is to provide academic programs for students whose career or personal circumstances limit their access to traditional forms of higher education. In keeping with this goal, the mission of the Extended Degree Programs is to provide educational opportunities for adult students to achieve their personal and career goals through non-traditional means.
    Students may use a combination of transfer credit, prior learning credit, learning packages, correspondence courses, telecourses and on-site classes in available locations to complete their degrees. A group format is available, called the cohort format, where students proceed through a degree program as a unit. Many cohorts are sponsored by a particular organization or group of organizations, which may select the students or allow participants to be self-selected. Cohorts are typically offered on-site at a

location chosen by the sponsor. Some degree programs offer the cohort format whenever a sufficient number of students sign up to pursue the degree as a group.

CHARTER OAK STATE COLLEGE

Contact:
Admissions Office
Charter Oak State College
270 Farmington Avenue
Farmington, Connecticut 06032-1934

Degrees Offered: Associate in Arts (A.A.), Associate in Science (A.S.), Bachelor of Arts (B.A.), Bachelor of Science (B.S.)

Summary: External degree program; faculty awards credits based on evaluation of transferred credit, non-collegiate sponsored instruction, tests and special assessment through portfolio review.

Fees:
Application Fee: $25
Enrollment Fee
      In-state residents: $314
      Out-of-state residents: $451
Baccalaureate Program (payable with application of approval of
      proposed baccalaureate program plan: $195
Annual Advisement and Records Maintenance Fee
      In-state residents: $220
      Out-of-state residents: $347
Portfolio Review
      In-state residents: $165
      Out-of-state residents: $248
      Special Course Evaluation: $75
Independent Guided Study
      In-state (per credit) $49
      Out-of-state (per credit) $72

Accreditation: Charter Oak State College functions under the administration and degree-granting authority of Connecticut's Board for State Academic Awards.

Residency: none

Narration:

Charter Oak is one of three state-sponsored colleges in the nation established to offer only external degree programs.

In this flexible program, a student may receive credit for course work completed at other regionally accredited institutions no matter how long ago the courses were taken. Credit may also be earned by university-sponsored correspondence courses, community college television courses, certain military school courses, some licensure and certification programs (especially in the health fields), various non-collegiate programs sponsored by business or other organizations, portfolio review and independent guided study.

The student may plan his/her own collegiate program and tailor the major areas of concentration to fit career and personal goals. The opportunity to pull together past credits from a variety of sources into a degree program allows motivated students to complete a degree in a shorter time with less expense.

In addition to a wide variety of liberal arts course offerings, a student may choose a concentration for a B.S. degree in Applied Science and Technology, Business, Computer Science, Fire Science Technology, Human Services, or Technology and Management.

CITY UNIVERSITY

Contact:
City University Administrative Offices
335 116th Avenue S.E.
Belleview, Washington 98004

Telephone:
206-637-1010
Toll free: 800-426-5596

FAX: 206-637-9689
Telex: 701080 CITY UNIV UD

Degrees Offered: Associate of Science (A.S.), Bachelor of Science (B.S.), Bachelor of Commerce (B.Comm.), Master of Business Administration (M.B.A.), Master of Public Administration (M.P.A.), Combined Master of Business Administration/Master of Public Administration (M.B.A./M.P.A.), Master of Education (M.Ed.).

Summary: Correspondence courses for a variety of undergraduate and graduate degree programs; credit by examination for prior learning

Fees:
Application fee: $50
Challenge Exam Fee: regular tuition + $300
Tuition:
Regular graduate per credit: $221
Undergraduate, regular upper-division per credit: $160
Undergraduate, regular lower-division per credit: $56

Accreditation: Northwest Association of Schools and Colleges

Residency: none

Narration:
Founded in Seattle in 1973, City University is a private institution designed to provide educational opportunities for segments of the population not being fully served through traditional processes. The Distance Learning Option makes available most of the university's degree and certificate programs entirely by independent study. Each course must be completed within a standard 10-week term if the student is studying within North America, or a 20-week term if the student is studying outside of North America. Course materials include a course outline, textbooks, bibliography, study problems, self-quizzes, assignments and readings. Students study independently, and follow the lessons and assignments outlined in the study guide. As the term proceeds, students and instructors remain in contact via mail, phone or computer link. Students must submit a mid-term and final exam, and in most courses a research paper is required. Distance learning

students pay standard tuition, are graded conventionally, and are eligible for some types of financial assistance.

A program of professionally directed independent travel-study is available at the undergraduate or graduate level. Independent study is offered in any academic discipline and may include (but is not limited to) special research projects, practicum or field work, and application projects. Travel-study programs are designed cooperatively by students and instructors to help assure that the travel experience yields maximum academic benefits.

The opportunity to obtain credit at City University by examination for prior learning is available through several nationally recognized standardized testing programs.

COLORADO STATE UNIVERSITY

Contact:
Colorado State University
Division of Continuing Education
Spruce Hall
Fort Collins, Colorado 80523

Telephone: 303-491-5288
Toll free: 800-525-4950
FAX: 303-491-7885

Degrees Offered: Master of Science (M.S.) in Agricultural Engineering, Chemical Engineering, Civil Engineering, Electrical Engineering, Mechanical Engineering, Environmental Engineering Program, Engineering Management Program, Industrial Engineering Program, Systems Engineering and Optimization Program, Computer Science, Industrial Sciences (Construction Management Program), Business Administration (Management Program), Statistics; Master of Business Administration (M.B.A.); Master of Education (M.Ed.) in Vocational Education (Human Resource Development Program); Doctor of Philosophy (Ph.D) in Agricultural Engineering, Chemical Engineering, Civil Engineering, Electrical Engineering, Mechanical Engineering, Environmental Engineering Program, Engineering Management Program,

Industrial Engineering Program, Systems Engineering and Optimization Program, Computer Science, Statistics

Summary: Graduate degree programs offered through videotape at designated corporate and public sites.

Fees:
Tuition
In-state: $300 per credit
Out-of-state (determined by site location): $300 per credit plus a $50 per credit fee
Many open sites collect a minimal fee to offset the expense of shipping tapes.

Accreditation: North Central Association of Colleges and Schools; Accrediting Board for Engineering and Technology

Residency: courses are offered via videotape at sites across the country

Narration:

The Colorado SURGE (State University Resources in Graduate Education) program delivers graduate education to working professionals who cannot attend on-campus classes. The SURGE program consists of regular on-campus courses taught by Colorado State graduate faculty which are videotaped in specially equipped classrooms. The tapes, along with handouts, are sent via UPS to participating sites. The sites make these tapes and materials available to students, provide information about the program, supply forms, proctor exams, and return the tapes. There are two different classifications of SURGE sites. Corporate sites are established by employers for their employees and are not open to the public. Open sites are established in cooperation with local public libraries and community colleges to serve the needs of students in the community at large; these are open to the public.

Interaction with the instructor is made possible through the use of electronic mail, fax, computer communication, surface mail, and telephone.

COLUMBIA PACIFIC UNIVERSITY

Contact:
Columbia Pacific University
1415 Third Street
San Rafael, California 94901

Telephone:
415-459-1650
Academic counselors: toll free: 800-227-0119;
Toll free in California: 800-552-5522
FAX: 415-459-5856
TELEX: 289773 CPUC UR

Degrees Offered: Bachelor of Arts (B.A.), Bachelor of Science
(B.S.), Master of Arts (M.A.), Master of Science (M.S.), Doctor of
Philosophy (Ph.D.), Doctor of Science (D.Sc.) offered through the
schools of: Arts and Sciences, Administration and Management,
Health and Human Services, International Law and Business.

Summary: Individualized non-resident Bachelor's, Master's, and
Doctoral Degree programs

Fees:
Registration fee: $200
Tuition per quarter: (slightly higher for students outside of the
U.S., U.K., and Canada)

Initial Enrollment Period	Thereafter
Bachelor's	$1,020 (four)
$340	
Master's	$1,070 (four)
$356	
Doctorate	$1,118 (four)
$373	
Bachelor's and Master's	
(with submatriculation*	$1,020 (two)
after two quarters)	$1,070 (four)
$356	

45

Master's and Doctorate
(with submatriculation* $1,070 (two)
after two quarters) $1,118 (four)
$373

*Submatriculation: a well qualified student may be permitted to begin work in a higher degree program before completing all of the requirements for graduation at the lower degree level.

Accreditation: none (granted "Full Institutional Approval" by the Superintendent of Public Instruction of the State of California)

Residency: none

Narration:

Columbia Pacific University is the largest non-resident graduate university in the United States. Its courses are taught by part-time adjunct faculty members who are highly qualified academics. The majority of them also hold faculty positions at other major institutions.

A student's extrainstitutional learning experience can be a source of academic credit. The term applies to learning acquired from work and life experiences, independent reading and study, the mass media, and participation in formal courses sponsored by associations, business, government, industry, the military, and unions. A student may also make use of papers, projects, or other materials previously developed to help fulfill the University's graduation requirements. The University will assign credit for properly documented learning experiences from a wide variety of career and academic sources.

Students may be accepted for enrollment at any time throughout the year. Students living anywhere in the world are accepted, as long as there is reliable postal and telephone service available. Whenever possible, the university will arrange for contacts with faculty living in the same area.

COLUMBIA UNIVERSITY/TEACHER'S COLLEGE

Contact:
Teacher's College, Columbia University
525 West 120 Street
Box 50
New York, New York 10027

Telephone:
212-678-3005
FAX: 212-678-4038

Degrees Offered: Doctor of Education (Ed.D.)

Summary: Doctorate program consisting of weekend classes and independent study; students must enroll for six complete semesters of study

Fees:
Tuition (per semester/summer session): $4,850

Accreditation: Northeastern Association of Schools and Colleges

Residency: Limited; required three-week summer session and weekend seminars during the year once a month

Narration:
The Adult Education Guided Independent Study (AEGIS) program is designed for a particular clientele: senior professionals with substantial experience in program development, administration of continuing education, staff development, human resources development and management, adult learning and training, who wish to earn a doctorate in education in three to five years. The program is geared to the interests of professionals who help adults learn in a variety of settings: universities and colleges, business and industry, health care institutions, public schools, community organizations, unions, libraries and museums, the armed forces, government agencies, vocational education and staff training programs, consulting organizations, international agencies, proprietary schools and the educational media.

Applicants must be prepared to enroll in seven semesters over two years of intensive course work and three additional semesters or more in which to complete and defend the dissertation. Each year of course work begins with an on-campus summer session scheduled for the last three weeks in June. Course work during the autumn and spring semesters includes participation in seminars on Friday evenings and Saturdays one weekend a month. A third summer session will help participants to further their dissertation research. Advisement is available throughout the academic year through electronic mail, fax, telephone, correspondence, and campus visits. Learning contracts and other course work can directly contribute to dissertation development. Participants receive extensive high-quality narrative feedback on their learning contracts and papers; there is no competitive grading in this program.

COLUMBIA UNION COLLEGE

Contact:
Columbia Union College
7600 Flower Ave.
Takoma Park, Maryland 20912-7796

Telephone:
301-891-4080
Toll free: 800-835-4212

Degrees Offered: Associate in Arts (A.A.) in General Studies; Bachelor of Arts (B.A.) in General Studies, Psychology, or Religion; Bachelor of Science (B.S.) in Business Administration

Summary: Seventh-Day Adventist college; External Degree program affiliated with Home Study International

Fees:
Application fee: $50

Accreditation: Middle States Association of Colleges and Schools

Residency: Limited

Narration:

The External Degree Program offers flexibility through its Directed Independent Study program. Under individualized faculty supervision and guidance, students study at home and prepare for proctored examinations. Course work may be started at any time during the year.

Students may earn credit for competencies and skills acquired through personal study, living and working in another culture, occupational experience, and home/community services.

HOME STUDY INTERNATIONAL

Contact:
Home Study International
12501 Old Columbia Pike
Silver Spring, Maryland 20904-6600

mailing address:
P.O. Box 4437
Silver Spring, Maryland 20914-4437

Degrees Offered: College credits are granted by Columbia Union College through an arrangement between their External Degree Program and Home Study International; see Columbia Union College for degree listings

Summary: Seventh-day Adventist distance education college

Fees:
Enrollment fee: $60
Tuition (per semester hour): $125

Accreditation: National Home Study Council (affiliate Columbia Union College is accredited by Middle States Association of Colleges and Schools

Residency: Limited

Narration:
Home Study International and Columbia Union College have enjoyed a close and mutually beneficial relationship for many years. Credit for college courses is granted through Columbia

Union College. Courses are offered in Business, Communications, Education, English, Fine Arts, Health and Nutrition, Geography, History, Languages, Psychology, Sociology, Religious Studies, and Science. Students may enroll for courses at any time during the year. Each course must be completed within 12 months from the date of enrollment.

COOK'S INSTITUTE OF ELECTRONIC ENGINEERING

Contact:
Cook's Institute of Electronics Engineering
4251 Cypress Drive
Jackson, Mississippi 39212

Telephone:
601-371-1351

Degrees Offered: Bachelor of Science in Electronics Engineering (B.S.E.E.); Master of Science (M.S.) in Computer Science or Electronics Engineering

Summary: Home study programs leading to degrees in electronics and computer science; no time limits for completion of courses.

Fees:
Total amount for complete 36-course program (B.S.E.E.): $6595
Financing is available

Accreditation: National Association of Private Nontraditional Schools and Colleges

Residency: none

Narration:
With advanced placement, a student may receive academic credit for previous schooling beyond the high school level. Credit also may be given for work experience as a professional electronic

technician to substitute for the lab work normally required for a B.S.E.E degree. The remaining courses can be completed without attending any residence classes in as little as 12 months.

Every Cook's Institute student has an academic field advisor. Communication between the students and the Institute is possible via mail and telephone. All study materials are exchanged by mail. Textbooks, audio-visual, audio-cassettes and other study materials are an essential core of Cook's Institute advanced degree programs. In the 36-course B.S.E.E. program the lesson material is supplemented with a set of 23 up-to-date engineering textbooks, supplied at no extra cost to the student. When new technology and developments occur in the electronics industry, graduates of the B.S.E.E. program may purchase individual new courses as they are developed at reduced cost.

The Master of Science in Electronics Engineering and Master of Science in computer Science programs are designed for the individual who is technically educated and has computer science and/or electronics engineering training or experience.

ECKERD COLLEGE

Contact:
Eckerd College
Program for Experienced Learners
4200 54th Avenue South
St. Petersburg, Florida 33711

Telephone:
813-864-8226
Toll free: 800-234-4735
FAX: 813-864-8422

Degrees Offered: Bachelor of Arts (B.A.), Bachelor of Science (B.S.) with majors in American Studies (History Track), Organizational Studies, Business Management, and Human Development

Summary: Liberal arts college related to the Presbyterian church with a values-centered general education program; some students permitted to complete degree requirements entirely through di-

51

rected/independent study courses.

Fees:

Application fee: $35

Degree plan development (upon submission of the plan of study; after completion of first course): $125

Portfolio Assessment: $210

Per course fee for prior experiential learning credit accepted: $60

Tuition (per course registration)

    Directed or independent study course: $545

    Comprehensive examination course, senior project or senior thesis: $545

Accreditation: Southern Association of Colleges and Schools

Residency: Limited. Required intensive weekend orientation workshop. Students in some majors are strongly urged to attend a 10-day on-campus senior component.

Narration:

    The Program for Experienced Learners recognizes the importance of relating general knowledge to special career and professional concerns. Students may select a major or an interdisciplinary concentration tailored to fit individual needs.

    A limited number of students are permitted to complete their degree requirements through directed study courses in the Extended Campus Program. These courses, prepared in advance by faculty members, usually require neither class participation nor attendance on campus. The student works independently under the direction of a faculty member, and communicates either by correspondence or telephone. For each course, a syllabus is provided, the reading and other research is defined, writing or other exercises are assigned, and the method of evaluation is specified. Independent study courses are initiated by the student to meet special interests or study opportunities; the content and format of the courses are determined by the supervising faculty member. Directed and independent studies are designed to be completed within 16 weeks, and may be started at any time.

    Students may be awarded college credit for a variety of learning experiences in non-academic settings, including: work experience, community activities, professional seminars/courses, previous college work, and other activities.

ELECTRONIC UNIVERSITY NETWORK

Contact:
Electronic University Network
1977 Colestin Road
Hornbrook, California 96044

Telephone:
Toll free: 800-22LEARN (225-3276), (Extension 1)

Degrees Offered: various undergraduate and graduate degrees (including Ph.D.)

Summary: Full degree programs offered directly by regionally accredited institutions through Electronic Campus, a national computer network.

Accreditation: Regionally accredited institutions are part of Electronic Campus.

Residency: none

Narration:
The Electronic Campus is accessible throughout the U.S. and Canada on America Online, a national computer network. Students use the America Online software (for MS-DOS, Macintosh, and Apple II computers) to sign on and participate in campus activities. The Electronic Campus lets students confer with instructors and other students, send and receive electronic mail, have private meetings with faculty, and do library research all from a personal computer with a modem.

EMBRY-RIDDLE AERONAUTICAL UNIVERSITY

Contact:
Embry-Riddle Aeronautical University
Department of Independent Studies
600 S. Clyde Morris Blvd.
Daytona Beach, Florida 32114-3900

Telephone:
904-226-6363
Toll free: 800-866-6271
FAX: 904-226-6949

Degrees Offered: Associate of Science (A.S.) in Professional Aeronautics, Bachelor of Science (B.S.) in Professional Aeronautics or Aviation Business Administration, Master of Aeronautical Science (M.A.S.)

Summary: Independent study program leading to standard undergraduate or graduate degree in aeronautics-related field.

Fees:
Application fee: $15
Tuition (per credit hour): $140
Video tapes:
      Rental: $20
      Purchase price: $70
Skytalk package for telemail courses: $20

Accreditation: Southern Association of Colleges and Schools

Residency: none

Narration:
     The programs are designed to enable the aviation/aerospace professional to master the application of modern management concepts, methods, and tools to the challenges of aviation and general business. The special intricacies of aviation are woven into a strong, traditional management foundation and examined in greater detail through the wide variety of electives. College credit is awarded in recognition of previous aviation training and profes-

54

sional experience.

The Independent Study program requires electronic interaction between faculty and students; therefore all students must have access to the following computer equipment:

1) IBM or compatible personal computer system with GRAPHIC capabilities,

2) Color or monochrome VGA monitor,

3) Hard drive system sufficient to load LOTUS and WORD PERFECT,

4) a 3.5 floppy drive,

5) Letter quality printer capable of printing GRAPHICS

6) A modem that will support between 300-2400 baud,

7) VCR and television for video tapes.

Course instructional materials consist of textbooks, study guides, audio cassette tapes, video tapes, or electronic mail. New terms begin each week and have a 15-week term period for completion. Enrollment in a new course can take place as soon as the student finishes with the previous class. Students are responsible for securing the services of an acceptable proctor who can administer mid-term and final exams.

EMPIRE STATE COLLEGE/STATE UNIVERSITY OF NEW YORK

Contact:
Center for Distance Learning
SUNY Empire State College
Two Union Avenue
Saratoga Springs, New York 12866-4390

Telephone:
518-587-2100

Degrees Offered: Associate and baccalaureate degrees in Business, Human Services, and Interdisciplinary Studies. Within the Business area, a baccalaureate in Fire Service Administration is available to residents of New York, Rhode Island, Pennsylvania, Vermont, New Hampshire, Massachusetts, Connecticut, Maine, and eastern Canada.

Summary: Courses and structured degree programs offered through mail, telephone and electronic media. Students are guided by an individual faculty mentor.

Fees:
Assessment fee (payable at time of first enrollment): $250
Tuition (degree seeking students) per credit: $90.35
Tuition (Non degree seeking students) per credit: $107.35
Students not residing in New York State are currently required to pay for telephone contacts with their tutors.

Accreditation: Middle States Association of Colleges and Schools

Residency: none

Narration:
Through the Center for Distance Learning, the College offers courses and structured degree programs that are accessible by telephone, mail, personal computer and other media, and require no face-to-face meetings. Guided independent study students are assigned to an individual faculty member who serves as mentor, giving guidance and support in all phases of college work. This mentor helps design learning contracts that outline the topics, learning activites and evaluative criteria for each 16-week term of study (beginning in September, January and May, with additional starting dates available). Learning contracts contain much the same information as a traditional course syllabus; however, the contract allows the student to make a variety of choices to suit individual needs and interests. Courses consist of carefully structured learning materials designed especially for adult independent study. Many of the courses are designed to enable adult students to incorporate their own learning from experience into their assignments. The course materials may include textbooks, workbooks, course guides, video programs, audio cassettes, computer programs and similar resources. Course tutors are specially prepared to work with students at a distance.

GEORGE WASHINGTON UNIVERSITY

Contact:
The George Washington University
The Educational Technology Leadership Program
Division of Continuing Education
2000 G Street, N.W.
Washington, D.C. 20052

Telephone:
202-994-6160
FAX: 202-994-4555

Degrees Offered: Master of Arts (M.A.) in Education (The Educational Technology Leadership Program)

Summary: Graduate program designed for professionals in education emphasizing the effect of high technology on the methods and content of education.

Fees:
Application fee: $45
Tuition (per credit hour): $550

Accreditation: Middle States Association of Colleges and Schools

Residency: none

Narration:
      The School of Education and Human Development has designed a graduate degree program to prepare people entering or advancing in schools, higher education, alternative educational environments, and other human service fields that use information systems. The Educational Technology Leadership Program provides students with opportunities to develop the knowledge, understanding, and skills necessary to become leaders in the dynamic new world of educational technology. This program has been specifically designed as a distance education program, with courses via television. Each course makes specific use of video, audio, print, and professional resources to meet the program objectives. The televised portion of the program includes demon-

strations, expert interviews, and question and answer sessions.

The Educational Technology Leadership Program is also available nationally by satellite and cable through Mind Extension University (ME/U): The Education Network. Registered students will receive textbooks and other printed materials through the mail and can communicate using electronic and voice mail. Designated portions of each course will be audio-interactive, and students are encouraged to call in on a toll-free line to participate in class discussions.

GEORGIA INSTITUTE OF TECHNOLOGY

Contact:
Georgia Institute of Technology
Atlanta, Georgia 30332-0240

Telephone:
404-894-3378
Toll free: 800-225-4656
FAX: 404-894-8924

Degrees Offered: Master of Science in Electrical Engineering (M.S.E.E.), Environmental Engineering, Health Physics/Radiological Engineering, Industrial Engineering, Nuclear Engineering; Doctor of Philosophy (Ph.D.). Computer Integrated Manufacturing Systems Certificate Program.

Summary: Technical graduate degree and certificate programs; video-based delivery system to off-campus students

Fees:
Tuition (per quarter credit hour): $195

Accreditation: The Environmental Engineering program is accredited by the Engineering Accreditation Commission of the Accreditation Board for Engineering and Technology.

Residency: none for most programs and courses; weekend seminars required for three courses

Narration:

Utilizing a video-based delivery system, Georgia Tech electronically extends the classroom to serve students who cannot attend on-campus. Students in the program have the flexibility to view lectures at times that fit their schedule. Video cameras record instructor presentations and student-instructor interactions during regular graduate classes. The videotapes and supporting materials are sent to off-campus students, who participate in classroom activities by watching the taped classes on video monitors at their place of work, their homes or at a designated location. Class tapes along with supplemental material will usually reach off-campus students within two to three days. At each off-campus location, a site coordinator must be identified to administer examinations.

The Master of Science in Health Physics/Radiological Engineering includes three courses with associated labs which require students to come to the campus for three 3-day weekends during the quarter or to have access to suitable equipment to perform the experiments.

The Computer Integrated Manufacturing Systems program offers an innovative approach to graduate education for students interested in identifying solutions to the manufacturing productivity problems facing U.S. industry. These problems are inherently multidisciplinary. Thus, students enrolled in the program pursue graduate degrees in a traditional academic discipline while fulfilling requirements for this multidisciplinary certificate. The program is designed to strike a balance between technical depth and broad comprehension of the problems facing industry and the current state of art for solving these problems.

GRACELAND COLLEGE

Contact:
Graceland College
700 College Avenue
Lamoni, Iowa 50140
or

Graceland College Outreach Program
Student Information Office
2203 Franklin Road, S.W.
P.O. Box 13486
Roanoke, Virginia 24034-3486

Telephone:
Toll free: 800-537-6276
FAX: 703-344-1508

Degrees Offered: Bachelor of Science (B.S.) in Nursing; Bachelor of Arts (B.A.) in Liberal Studies

Summary: Outreach program designed to allow working R.N.s to complete baccalaureate degrees at home

Fees:
Application fee: $60
Tuition (per semester hour): $215. Minimum registration 2 courses, 6 semester hours

Accreditation: National League for Nursing

Residency: Limited; one or two 2-week residency sessions are required (6 or 7 credit hours each); clinical components of some nursing courses may be completed in the student's own community under the direction of college-approved preceptors.

Narration:
During the independent study phase of the program, the student registers for a set of two or more courses at a time and is assigned an instructor for each course. Resource materials are shipped via United Parcel Service, consisting of the required texts, a learning guide developed by a member of the faculty, and instructional video tapes. Course requirements typically include unit assignments, projects, tests, and a proctored final examination. The instructor is available for toll-free telephone consultations. A six month time period is allowed for completion of each set of courses.

Students may come to campus for their clinical experience, or may utilize a college-approved preceptor in the home community to monitor progress in the required clinical courses. Students enrolled in the B.A.-Liberal Studies program may receive up to 64 semester hours of credit through evaluation of their nursing education and experience. There are no restrictions on how long ago a course may have been completed for it to be considered for credit. A total of 75 semester hours of credit may be transferred from a community college.

The Liberal Studies program offers the R.N. the opportunity to design an individualized academic program that builds on his/her previous education and professional background. Two concentrations are offered via independent study: Health Care Administration and Health Care Psychology.

GRANTHAM COLLEGE OF ENGINEERING

Contact:
Grantham College of Engineering
34641 Grantham College Road
Slidell, Louisiana 70460

mailing address:
P.O. Box 5700
Slidell, Louisiana 70469-5700

Telephone:
504-649-4191

Degrees Offered: Associate of Science in Engineering Technology (A.S.E.T.), Bachelor of Science in Engineering Technology (B.S.E.T.)

Summary: Degree programs with major emphasis in electronics or computers

Fees:
Total price for B.S.E.T. program: $9,000 (deferred payment plan is slightly higher)
Each of the four phases: $2250
Cost includes registration fee, all lesson materials and required

reference books, a 16-bit microprocessor trainer, all grading and consultation services, and the awarding of the degrees earned.

Accreditation: National Home Study Council

Residency: none

Narration:

The degree programs are designed for part-time study by students who find it impractical to attend regular college classes. The purpose is to teach theoretical and practical aspects of the major and supporting subjects, from beginning concepts to the bachelor degree level. A part-time independent home-study student should complete each of the four phases of the program in 12-24 months. The mid-phase and end-of-phase examinations must be proctored by a responsible official.

Distance education includes printed lessons (written by the Grantham technical staff and including some standard texts sent to the student), completed tests sent by the student to the college for grading and comment, and various kinds of communication between the student and his instructors regarding the home-study lessons and tests.

The electronics program is designed for those students who have worked and/or are now working as electronics technicians or in similar jobs, or expect to be working in such jobs. The electronics program is based on the presumption that the student either already has or will obtain, on his own, proficiency in the operation of test equipment, hand tools, etc., which is normally learned in laboratory courses or by personal experimentation or on-the-job experience.

In the computer program, practical application work is included in the lessons, and operating practice accumulated as a byproduct of doing the lessons leads to improved skill as well as knowledge.

GREENWICH UNIVERSITY

Contact:
Greenwich University

103 Kapiolani Street
Hilo, Hawaii

Mailing address:
P.O. Box 1717
Hilo, Hawaii 96721 U.S.A.

Telephone:
From the U.S. and Canada:
Toll free: 800-367-4465
From other countries or Hawaii:
808-935-9934
FAX: 808-969-7469

Degrees Offered: Bachelor's, Master's, and Doctoral degrees

Summary: Flexible, self-paced programs in which students become actively involved in organizing their own knowledge and experiences

Fees:
Bachelor's degree program: $3,000
Master's degree program: $2,500
Doctorate program: $3,500

Accreditation: currently undergoing the accreditation process with the Pacific Association for Schools and Colleges

Residency: none

Narration:
Greenwich offers two approaches to earning degrees. One is basically a highly individualized program, tailored to each student's interests, abilities, wishes and needs, as tempered by faculty input and core curriculum requirements. The other is a more structured curriculum, where all study materials are packaged and pre-structured. Each student is matched with one or more faculty mentors, and together they develop a Learning Contract—a course of study which may include readings, writings, papers, discussions, and a practicum.

All disciplines are divided into three main areas of study:

Professional Studies, including those that may require state certification as a prerequisite for professional practice. These include: Education, Nursing, Counseling, Psychology, Social Work, Business, Management/Administration, Law, Environmental Sciences, Women's Studies and Computer Sciences. Scientific Studies emphasize scientific methodologies in the natural and social sciences, such as: Physical Science, Geology, Physics, Astronomy, Biology, Botany, Political Science, Sociology, Anthropology and Psychology. Liberal Arts include: Fine Arts, Applied Arts, Aesthetics, Music, Humanities, Speech, Philosophy, Journalism, Linguistics, Literature, Languages, English, Religion and History.

HENLEY MANAGEMENT COLLEGE

Contact:
Henley Management College
Greenlands
Henley-on-Thames
Oxfordshire RG9 3AU
England

Telephone:
0491-571454
FAX: 0491-571635
International:+44-491-571454
Telex: 849026 Henley G

Degrees Offered: Master's of Business Administration (M.B.A.) and Diploma in Management

Summary: Comprehensive business and management programs through distance learning

Fees:
(Cost is approximate depending on current exchange rate)
Distance Learning M.B.A.: Total $9825

Accreditation: Royal Charter

Residency: none

Narration:

The M.B.A. is a three stage course which covers the key areas of study relevant to all managers: operations, people, markets, information and resources. It is based on specially developed work books, videos, audio materials and an innovative Computer Mediated Communication system that puts all course members on-line to a global learning network. This enables them to access data, exchange information and take part in electronic conferencing. This system provides electronic tutorials for course members who cannot easily reach a study center; convenient access to subject tutors for problem-solving, the latest information on course content, design and administration; access to external services and databases to aid project and assignment work; and the ability to participate in interactive conferences on course subjects. Questions on course material are answered through a 24-hour help line that gives direct access to M.B.A. staff. The College provides a comprehensive range of support services, which are available anywhere in the world.

Optional workshops provide an opportunity for course members to meet with tutors and exchange ideas with their peers. These are held at Henley and at other centers on the Henley M.B.A. Network.

HOFSTRA UNIVERSITY

Contact:
University Without Walls
at New College
Hofstra University
Hempstead, New York 11550

Telephone:
516-463-5820

Degrees Offered: Bachelor of Arts (B.A.), Master of Arts (M.A.) in

Interdisciplinary Studies

Summary: Flexible, individualized liberal arts program with limited residency

Fees:
Application fee: $25
Acceptance fee: $100 payable upon acceptance; credited toward first registration
Full contract tuition: $2360
    Fee: $30
Half contract tuition: $1180
    Fee: $30
Informal Prior Learning:
  Assessment Fee, Full Graduation Requirement: $690
    Fee: $30
  Assessment Fee, Half graduation requirement: $345
    Fee: $30
Undergraduate tuition (per semester hour): $342
New College per semester (12-20 semester hours): $5520

Accreditation: Middle States Association of Schools and Colleges

Residency: Limited; must have access to the university once a month

Narration:
    The first New College was founded in 1379 at Oxford University in Great Britain for masters and apprentices seeking intellectual freedom from the constraints of that time and place. The New College at Hofstra is a small college within the larger university, offering individualized and flexible Bachelors and Masters degrees in liberal arts. Areas of study are: Creative Studies, Humanities, Interdisciplinary Studies, Natural Sciences, and Social Sciences.
    The University Without Walls Program offers independent study through contract learning. Independent study is work done outside the traditional classroom on a one-to-one basis with a faculty member. The contract is the written agreement between the university, the student and the faculty supervisor that guides the independent study project. Most often, contract learning

involves library research, field research, internships in professional settings or in artistic/performance settings. Students have their performance evaluated on a pass/fail basis.

Academic credit for undergraduate learning which has occurred before entrance to the University takes two forms. Advanced standing is granted for formal prior learning. Students also have the opportunity to have informal prior learning assessed for credit, including programs offered by institutes, continuing education organizations or even unaccredited colleges. Also, students may request examinations to obtain credit for prior life experiences that have liberal arts value.

INDIANA INSTITUTE OF TECHNOLOGY

Contact:
Indiana Institute of Technology
Extended Studies Division
1600 East Washington Blvd.
Fort Wayne, Indiana 46803

Telephone:
219-422-5561
Toll free: 800-288-1766

Degrees Offered: Associate of Science (A.S.) in Business Administration; Bachelor of Science (B.S.) in Business Administration

Summary: Independent study undergraduate degree programs in business topics

Fees:
Application fee: $50
Tuition, including textbooks (per semester hour): $160
Life Experience Assessment Fee (per semester hour): $20

Accreditation: North Central Association of Colleges and Schools

Residency: none

Narration:

The Independent Study Program offers the opportunity to complete an entire college degree without attending formal classes. The student is provided with the necessary course materials via mail, along with faculty home and work phone numbers so that the student may contact them as needed. A Modular Academic Package is utilized in place of the professor's lecture. It instructs students as to the homework assignments and supplements course material where the textbook may be deficient to prepare students for exams. Prior to graduation, students must demonstrate their competency by supervised written examinations and/ or written compositions.

The Associate of Science Degree has two concentration options: finance or management. The Bachelor of Science Degree offers students the choice of four concentration areas: finance, management, marketing or human resources.

An important component of the Extended Studies Division is the recognition of education gained outside the formal classroom. This includes knowledge acquired through seminars, corporate training, military service, self-study and many other ways. The process by which a student earns credit for life experience begins with a foundation course for the procedures designed to guide students through the steps leading to the completion and submission of a written Portfolio of Life Experiences. When completed, students submit their portfolio for faculty review. Credit may also be awarded through successful performance on standardized examinations.

INDIANA UNIVERSITY

Contact:
Indiana University
Division of Extended Studies
Owen Hall 001
Bloomington, Indiana 47405-5201

Telephone:
812-855-5792

Toll free:
 Nationwide (except Indiana, Alaska, and Hawaii): 800-334-1011
 Indiana: 800-342-5410
FAX: 812-855-8680
Internet E-mail: EXTEND@INDIANA.EDU

Degrees Offered: Associate of General Studies; Bachelor of General Studies

Summary: Undergraduate degree program by correspondence; credit granted for life experiences, noncollegiate training, and proficiency exams. Large number of correspondence courses offered

Fees:
Application fee: $25
Tuition (per credit hour): $74

Accreditation: North Central Association of Colleges and Schools

Residency: none

Narration:
 The Division of Extended Studies is composed of two major programs: Independent Study by Correspondence and the General Studies Degree. Independent study is an individualized instructional service; the student may enroll at any time of the year, decide how to pace the program of study, and when to take examinations. One year is allowed for completion of a course. Examinations must be taken in the presence of a qualified supervisor. The University offers more than 200 college-level correspondence courses.
 The General Studies Degree Program brings a college education to those who have been prevented from beginning or completing work in a traditional degree program because of work schedules, domestic responsibilities, or logistical problems. The program enables students to complete an associate degree or a bachelor's degree in general studies at their own pace and their own location. Course work consists of a core of arts and sciences courses—humanities, social and behavioral sciences, mathematics, sciences, and a wide range of electives. Degree requirements

may be completed in a variety of ways, allowing students to design a flexible program of study tailored to their backgrounds and needs. The program recognizes that students gain college-level knowledge and understanding through various life experiences that are equivalent to the subject matter of specific courses in the university curriculum. Credit may also be granted for proficiency examinations, educational programs in noncollegiate organizations, correspondence courses, and military service programs.

INSTITUTE FOR ADVANCED STUDY OF HUMAN SEXUALITY

Contact:
Institute for Advanced Study of Human Sexuality
1523 Franklin Street
San Francisco, California 94109

Degrees Offered: Master of Human Sexuality; Doctor of Education (Ed.D.); Doctor of Philosophy (Ph.D.). Certificate programs in Clinical Sexology, Sex Therapy, Forensic Sexology and Erotology

Summary: Limited-residency graduate degree programs in the field of human sexuality

Fees:
Tuition, full enrollment (per trimester) $2,500 or $7,500 per year
Certificate costs:
Clinical Sexology: $3,000
Sex Therapy: $1,500
Forensic Sexology: $1,500
Erotology: $1,500
Assoc. in Sexology: $2,200
AIDS/STD Prevention: $1,400

Residency: Limited

Narration:
    The Institute offers four graduate degree programs for

persons wishing academic training in the field of human sexuality. These programs are designed specifically for persons who intend to make the field of human sexuality a major focus in their professional careers. The Master's degree is a step toward professional qualification in the field of human sexuality and may be sufficient in many situations, such as teaching about human sexuality in public schools. The Doctor of Education degree offers a broad background in the field for those who wish to become educators and/or generalists. This degree has particular relevance for those who may teach courses, design educational programs or utilize writing, filmmaking or other communication media as their form of service in human sexuality. The Doctor of Human Sexuality is for those with a background in therapy or counseling. The Doctor of Philosophy requires an analytical, original and independent investigation. The Institute will give a limited amount of credit for previous academic work and professional experience in the field of human sexuality.

Graduates of the Institute are teachers in high schools, colleges and medical schools. Many are in private practice as therapists, while others combine therapy with teaching and workshops. Some graduates have continued in their previous professions, as clergy, social workers, researchers, psychiatrists and physicians, but now do specialized work in sexology.

Students can expect to spend two to three weeks per trimester at the Institute in order to fulfill practica and lecture requirements. Some courses are available on videotape which can be sent to students at home by special arrangement.

INTERNATIONAL CORRESPONDENCE SCHOOLS/ CENTER FOR DEGREE STUDIES

Contact:
National Education Corporation
Independent Study
925 Oak Street
Scranton, Pennsylvania 18515

Degrees Offered: Associate in Specialized Business (A.S.B.) in Accounting, Applied Computer Science, Hospitality Management, and Business Management; Associate in Specialized Technology (A.S.T.) degree in Civil, Electrical, Industrial, and Mechanical Engineering, and Electronics Technologies

Summary: Career degrees by correspondence study in specialized disciplines

Fees:
Course prices are listed for the first semester only and range from $689-$789
Life/Work Portfolio Evaluation fee: $100

Accreditation: National Home Study Council

Residency: none

Narration:

The Center for Degree Studies is a nontraditional proprietary institution offering postsecondary career education in business and technology. Established to provide a learning system based on guided independent study, the Center aims to provide specialized education designed to fulfill practical needs—career, job advancement, self-improvement—without sacrificing the ultimate goals of education: personal growth and enrichment. In support of its philosophy, the Center seeks to satisfy the need of adults for career-oriented college-level education without seriously disrupting established life patterns.

In addition to the course materials provided, students are encouraged to make full use of all supplemental learning resources available to them including public, private, and professional libraries and research facilities. A hot line, available throughout the continental U.S., is available for help with correspondence lessons.

A degree candidate completing all lessons for a given semester with an acceptable academic performance will be eligible to take the required proctored final examination. There will be four open-book proctored final examinations, one for each of the four semesters of work. Each comprehensive examination will test the candidate on all courses completed in the semester covered.

Students may submit the names of potential proctor candidates for approval.

═══

INTERNATIONAL SCHOOL OF INFORMATION MANAGEMENT

Contact:
International School of Information Management
University Business Center
130 Cremona Drive
Santa Barbara, California 93117-2360

Mailing address: ISIM
P.O. Box 1999
Santa Barbara, California 93116-1999

Telephone:
805-685-1500
FAX: 805-685-9685
Toll free: 800-441-ISIM (441-4746)

Degrees Offered: Master of Science in Information Resources Management or Master of Business Administration in Information Resources Management

Summary: Distance learning graduate programs in information technology delivered by interactive computer "electronic classroom"

Fees:
Tuition (per unit; three weeks of education/training): $345

Accreditation: National Home Study Council

Residency: none

Narration:
       The School's mission is to provide working adults with flexible opportunities for study of both business and information

resources management, to enable them to meet the needs of their organization through the effective integration of business management objectives and information systems design and delivery. The programs focus on information, its strategic uses, and its effective management. They are directed at adult learners who seek to further their education without having to neglect their work or their family obligations.

The School provides courses and seminars in Information Resources Management, which includes subjects in Information Systems and Technology, Telecommunications, Computer Sciences and Management, in addition to certificate programs in Telecommunications and Computer Technologies. Credit courses and non-credit courses are offered in the following five subject areas: Telelearning/Teletraining; Telecommunications; Computer Technology; Information Resources Management; and Business Administration with an Information Resources Management focus.

Courses are delivered via a computer conferencing network that provides interactive exchanges between faculty and students. Each student and faculty member has an electronic "mailbox" that serves as the channel for interaction with the network. The faculty member who teaches the course provides general instruction and individual assistance, and encourages participation in student/faculty and student/student discussions. Courses are small, often fewer than ten. Learners are independent and are encouraged to conduct their studies in the context of their work environment. They are free to work at their own pace: communication via computer with their teachers gives them time for deliberation before they go online with their questions or answers. Delivered asynchronously (at sender's and receiver's convenience), these courses provide convenience and flexibility for adult learners.

IOWA STATE UNIVERSITY

Contact:
Iowa State University of Science and Technology
College of Agriculture

Off-campus Programs in Professional Agriculture
20 Curtiss Hall
Ames, Iowa 50011-1050

Telephone:
515-294-9666
Toll free: 800-747-4478
FAX: 515-294-5334

Degrees Offered: Bachelor of Science (B.S.) and Master of Agriculture (M.A.G.)

Summary: Agriculture degree programs for off-campus students

Fees:
Tuition
  Undergraduate (per credit): $92
  Graduate (per credit): $145
Video purchase and lab fees may be required

Accreditation: North Central Association of Colleges and Schools

Residency: Limited; some workshops and lab sessions may be required

Narration:
The course of study for the Bachelor of Science degree encompasses three major areas: animal ecology and sciences, agricultural social sciences and economics, and plant and soil sciences.

The Master of Agriculture program is ideal for farmers and agribusiness people with bachelor's degrees who want to upgrade their professional education. It combines core courses with a program of individual interest. The creative component demonstrates independent activity by means of a written report of laboratory, field, or library research. The curriculum is considered to be a professional master's degree, not preparation for a Ph.D. degree, and a thesis option is not available.

Courses for the degrees include livestock housing, pest management, turfgrass management, crop conditioning and handling, soil management, plant and animal breeding, ruminant

75

and non-ruminant nutrition, ag law, farm management, ag marketing and others. These courses are offered via videotape, satellite, and face-to-face instruction at various sites in Iowa. Students must be able to travel to Ames for at least four workshop credit hours for the master's program. Bachelor's degree candidates must come to Ames to take two workshop credit hours and must also participate in a one-day on-campus orientation. Most videotape classes also require on-campus lab sessions, usually on Saturdays. Students correspond with the instructors by mail, toll-free phone calls, e-mail, or fax.

KANSAS STATE UNIVERSITY

Contact:
Kansas State University
Non-Traditional Study
Division of Continuing Education
College Court Building
Manhattan, Kansas 66506-6002

Telephone:
913-532-5687
FAX: 913-532-5637

Degrees Offered: Bachelor of Science (B.S.) in Social Science, or Animal Sciences and Industry

Summary: Degree programs offered through Mind Extension University cable network

Fees:
Application fee: $25
Tuition (per 3-credit course): $450

Accreditation: North Central Association of Colleges and Schools

Residency: none

Narration:

76

Courses are delivered by Mind Extension University by cable, satellite and videotape to the home or workplace. Students enroll in college courses through the Mind Extension University Education Center and watch the video component of the classroom lectures. Students complete assignments, take proctored examinations, and work with a university faculty member from the convenience of their home or job, receiving credit from Kansas State University.

The Social Science degree is concerned with the study of human behavior, interrelationships and institutions. It is open only to individuals pursuing a first bachelor's degree. Courses for the degree in Animal Sciences and Industry give instruction in selection, breeding, feeding, management, and marketing of beef and dairy cattle, horses, poultry, sheep and swine, as well as instruction in the processing and use of the products these animals provide.

LESLEY: THE GRADUATE SCHOOL

Contact:
Lesley College Graduate School
Office of Admissions
29 Everett Street
Cambridge, Massachusetts 02138-2790

Telephone:
617-349-8454
Toll free: 800-999-1959, ext. 8300

Degrees Offered: Bachelor of Science (B.S.;) Bachelor of Arts in Behavioral Science (B.A. in B.S.); Master of Arts (M.A.), Master of Education (M.Ed.); Certificate of Advanced Graduate Study (C.A.G.S.) in Independent Study

Summary: Independent study and limited-residency programs; individually-designed majors

Fees:
Degree candidates are assessed one tuition fee for a plan of study

that is completed in three to six semesters ($11,000)

Accreditation: New England Association of Schools and Colleges

Residency: Limited

Narration:

The Independent Study Degree Program is designed for men and women whose field of study is non-traditional or interdisciplinary, for people who cannot attend course-based on- or off-campus programs, or whose unique professional or personal situations make systematic independent study their preferred mode of education. Each student's program is unique and is based on a Study Plan that is developed by the student as part of the application process. The initial plan includes goals, learning and documentation methods, and ideas for the preparation of a final project. Learning methods include a combination of activities appropriate to the student's field of interest, such as tutorials, directed reading, coursework, fieldwork, practica, or apprenticeships. Students carry out their graduate studies over a period of one to three years, with advisement from a team of three faculty members with whom the student meets four times during the program. On-campus attendance at a one-day colloquium in the Fall is recommended. Credit may be awarded for extensive work experience and life skills related to the student's future career; and for academic proficiency demonstrated on standardized examinations.

The Intensive Residency Option program permits mature, motivated students to carry a full undergraduate academic program while continuing work and family responsibilities. Bachelor of Science and Bachelor of Arts in Behavioral Science degree programs alternate two intensive residency periods each calendar year with individually guided, independent study. During ten-day residencies, students attend study skills workshops, choose faculty advisors, plan their individually guided study projects for the coming six months, and participate in social and cultural activites. Between residencies, students prepare independent study projects with careful guidance from faculty advisors and help from consultants and field supervisors as needed. Students in this program combine a wide range of disciplines to shape their own specializations.

LIBERTY UNIVERSITY

Contact:
Liberty University
School of LifeLong Learning
Box 11803
Lynchburg, Virginia 24506-9978

Telephone:
Toll free: 800-424-9595
800-228-7354 (admissions)

Degrees Offered: Associate of Arts (A.A.) in General Studies or Religion; Bachelor of Science (B.S.) in Business, Psychology, Biblical Foundations, Interdisciplinary Studies, General Studies, Church Ministries; Master of Arts (M.A.) in Professional Counseling or Religion

Summary: Christian college offering undergraduate and graduate degrees in interdisciplinary and Christian-related topics

Fees:
New Student Registration: $60
Course General Fee: $45
Textbook Fee: $60

Accreditation: Southern Association of Colleges and Schools

Residency: Limited; up to four one-week residencies

Narration:
Liberty University consists of seven colleges and schools. The External Degree Program is specifically designed for busy working adults who need a flexible class schedule. Class lectures for each course are mailed to the student on videocassettes along with detailed study notes and textbooks. Faculty and staff are available via a toll-free phone number to offer step-by-step assistance through degree requirements and class schedules. Students may interact with university professors whenever questions arise, either through a toll-free phone system, or through personal computer and modem communication with the professor's per-

sonal computer. Residency requirements can be met by attending week-long, on-campus modulars during the summer months and/or during selected holidays.

College credit may be awarded for military training, schooling and experience, and for successful performance on a special examination in a given subject area. Credit may also be given by special application for work experience, community service and special accomplishments.

LOMA LINDA UNIVERSITY

Contact:
Loma Linda University
School of Public Health
Extended Programs
Nichol Hall 1706
Loma Linda, California 92354

Telephone:
909-824-4595
Toll free: 800-854-5661

Degrees Offered: Master of Public Health (M.P.H.)

Summary: Graduate program for health professionals offered in intensive sessions at various locations around the country

Fees:
Tuition (per unit):
Regular credit: $285
Audit: $145

Accreditation: Western Association of Schools and Colleges, Council on Education for Public Health

Residency: Instructors travel to various sites in the United States to meet with students in an intensive three-day class session.

Narration:

The Extended Program at the School of Public Health offers a unique and practical way for mid-career health professionals to obtain a Master of Public Health degree while maintaining their present employment. The format includes a combination of independent study (pre- and post-lecture assignments) and intensive student/instructor contact. The student is not required to spend time on campus, rather instructors travel to various sites in the United States to meet with students in an intensive three-day class session. One class per quarter is taught at each site. The program is geared to the needs of physicians, dentists, nurses, and other health professionals desiring to become qualified to organize health programs, and to engage in health promotion activities. Two majors are available: Health Promotion and Health Administration.

LOYOLA UNIVERSITY

Contact:
Loyola University
Institute for Ministry
Box 67
6363 St. Charles Avenue
New Orleans, Louisiana 70118

Telephone:
504-865-3728
Toll free: 800-777-5469

Degrees Offered: Master of Religious Education (M.R.E.), Master of Pastoral Studies (M.P.S.)

Summary: Catholic (Jesuit) university offering ministerial education

Fees:
Application fee: $20
Graduate tuition (per credit hour): $397
All students earning credit automatically receive 50% discount
Non-credit courses (per credit hour): $70

Accreditation: Southern Association of Colleges and Schools

Residency: limited

Narration:

The Institute for Ministry began in 1968 as "the Catechetical Institute of New Orleans" at Notre Dame Seminary under the auspices of the Archdiocese of New Orleans. In 1978, the Institute moved to nearby Loyola University and became a part of the University's program of graduate studies. It became an important educational center for carrying out the renewal mandated by the Second Vatican Council concerning the expanded participation of laity in the Church's ministry. Religious educators and pastoral ministers enrolled in summer courses, some for continuing education and some in pursuit of master's degrees in religious education or pastoral studies.

The 30-hour master's programs are led by Loyola-trained and supervised facilitators. The facilitators utilize printed course manuals and videotapes as well as peer group reflection in a structured process. The program is designed to provide in-depth information and reflection on the theory and skills appropriate to persons in a variety of ministerial roles.

MARYWOOD COLLEGE

Contact:
Marywood College
Office of The Off-Campus Degree Program
Scranton, Pennsylvania 18509

Telephone:
717-348-6211
Toll free: 800-836-6940
FAX: 717-348-0459

Degrees Offered: Bachelor of Science (B.S.) in Accounting or Business Administration

Summary: Catholic college offering off-campus bachelor's degrees in business

Fees:
Application fee: $40
Registration Fee (3 credits): $35; (4 or more credits): $60
Tuition (per credit): $75

Accreditation: Middle States Association of Colleges and Schools

Residency: Limited; two 2-week intensive residencies are required

Narration:
Marywood College is an independent Catholic college. The Off-Campus Degree Program is a system of education designed to meet the special needs of adults through individual, guided study. Students have daily access to campus faculty through telecommunications. The "teacher" is not a single individual but rather a composite of researchers, authors, intructors, testing specialists, and practitioners in accounting, business administration, and the liberal arts who collaborate on the instruction units.

Students are encouraged to make full use of all supplemental learning resources available to them, including public, private and professional libraries and research facilities. Final examinations must be monitored by a proctor who has a master's degree or higher. Credit may be granted for prior learning acquired by experience.

MIND EXTENSION UNIVERSITY

Contact:
Mind Extension University
Education Center
9697 East Mineral Avenue
P.O. Box 3309
Englewood, Colorado 80155-3309

Telephone:
303-792-3111

Toll free: 800-777-MIND (800-777-6463)
FAX: 303-799-0966

Degrees Offered: Bachelor of Arts (B.A.), Bachelor of Science (B.S.), Master of Arts (M.A.), Master of Business Administration (M.B.A.)

Summary: Network of courses and degree programs from 24 public and private colleges and universities delivered by cable/satellite television or video tape

Fees: Established separately by each of the colleges and universities in the network

Accreditation: All degrees, programs and courses offered in the network are supported by universities and colleges holding regional accreditation

Residency: none

Narration:

The Mind Extension University brings college courses into homes and/or the workplace via cable/satellite television or video tape. The network includes 24 accredited public and private colleges and universities.

The affiliate schools develop and evaluate courses and provide academic support. The Mind Extension University delivers programming, provides administrative support and offers student services through the Education Center, which links students and universities through the cable network. Students can complete course work anywhere without residency requirements in the United States; some programs are offered internationally.

Undergraduate level degree completion programs are as follows:

Bachelor's Degree in Management from University of Maryland University College

Bachelor of Arts in Social Sciences from Washington State University

Bachelor of Science in Interdisciplinary Social Science from Kansas State University

Bachelor of Science in Animal Sciences and Industry from Kansas State University

Bachelor of Science in Business Administration from Regis University

Graduate level degree programs are as follows:

Master of Business Administration from Colorado State University

Master of Arts in Education and Human Development from the George Washington University

Master of Arts in Library Science from the University of Arizona

Certificate programs offer personal and professional advancement at the graduate level:

Early Reading Instruction Certificate from the University of Colorado at Colorado Springs

Teaching At-risk Learners Certificate from Washington State University

Quality Improvement Certificate from Colorado State University

Not-for-credit topics include adult education and literacy, GED, international language and culture, career hour and more.

MOUNT SAINT VINCENT UNIVERSITY

Contact:
Mount Saint Vincent University
Halifax, Nova Scotia
Canada B3M 2J6
or
Open Learning, EMF Center, Room 121
Mount Saint Vincent University
Halifax, Nova Scotia B3M 2J6

Telephone:
902-457-6511
Toll free: 800-665-3838
FAX: 902-457-2618

Degrees Offered: Degree in Tourism and Hospitality Management, Certificate in Business Administration, plus other courses in mathematics, economics and writing.

Summary: Limited number of certificate and degree programs and elective courses offered through distance learning modes

Fees:
Application fee: $25
Course fee:
> Each half-unit: $340
> One-unit course: $660
> One-and-a-half units: $965

Residency: none

Narration:
> The Open Learning program focuses on new and innovative approaches to distance education, providing university courses to students who cannot come to campus due to responsibilities or constraints of distance or time. Courses are delivered with a print-base and may be complemented by telephone, television, workshops, computer assisted learning, audio/video cassettes, and teleconference seminars.
> The Degree in Tourism and Hospitality Management has been designed to answer the need for university-educated professionals in this field, and students meet all the same requirements as on-campus students. This degree is recognized across Canada and the United States.
> Open Learning also offers a Certificate in Business Administration, as well as elective courses in Finite Mathematics, Probability and Statistics, and Writing Theory and Practice.

NEW YORK INSTITUTE OF TECHNOLOGY

Contact:
New York Institute of Technology
On-line Campus

Distance Learning Program
P.O. Box 8000
Old Westbury, New York 11568-8000

Telephone:
516-686-7712
Toll free: 800-222-6948
FAX: 516-484-8327

Degrees Offered: Bachelor of Arts (B.A.) in Interdisciplinary Studies; Bachelor of Science (B.S.) in Interdisciplinary Studies, Business Administration (Management Option) or Behavioral Sciences (Options: Psychology, Sociology, Community Mental Health and Criminal Justice); Bachelor of Professional Studies in Interdisciplinary Studies

Summary: Degree programs by computer conferencing method

Fees:
Application fee: $30
Start-up fee: $75
Tuition (per credit hour): $260

Accreditation: Middle States Association of Colleges and Schools

Residency: none

Narration:
      The Institute's On-Line campus (formerly known as the American Open University) offers degrees to students seeking a non-traditional approach to undergraduate education, making college courses possible for students who choose not to attend classes on a conventional campus. Communication between students and faculty takes place entirely over a computer conferencing network, so that the course work is done by students and faculty exchanging text messages on computer screens. This conferencing does not have to be done at the same time. To log on to computer conferencing a student needs 1) either a Macintosh or MS-DOS (or PC-DOS) IBM or IBM-compatible computer, preferably with a hard disk drive to provide large storage and rapid access to data; 2) any Hayes-compatible modem operating at 1200 or

2400 BPS; 3) Procomm or PC Plus (or Microphone for Macintosh) communications software; and 4) any compatible printer.

The Institute offers a variety of means for recognizing prior experience including transfer of credit, nationally approved examinations, assessment of prior learning in military and corporate training programs, and portfolio development. However, a minimum of thirty credit hours must be taken with the Institute to complete a degree.

NEWPORT UNIVERSITY

Contact:
Newport University
2220 University Drive
Newport Beach, California 92660

Telephone:
714-631-1155
FAX: 714-631-0555

Degrees Offered: Associate in Arts (A.A.), Bachelor of Arts (B.A.) offered through the schools of Business Administration, Education and the Department of Human Behavior; Bachelor of Science (B.S.) in Engineering; Master of Science (M.S.) in School of Engineering; Juris Doctor Degree (J.D.) awarded by the School of Law. Master's and Doctoral Degrees are awarded in Business Administration, Education, Human Behavior, Psychology and Religion.

Summary: Flexible degree programs emphasizing the student's interests and life experiences

Fees:
Application fee: $35
Tuition: (per unit): $70
Change of program fee: $100

Accreditation: Institutional approval by the Council for Private Postsecondary and Vocational Education

Residency: none

Narration:

Newport University was developed as a scholarly alternative to traditional institutions of higher education. It is committed to the idea that each individual is a unique and diverse person, and that society will benefit to the extent that each individual is able to add to the social pool of talent and competence if given the opportunity to develop personal skills and knowledge. The purpose of the University is to provide educational programs leading to academic degrees for individuals who have demonstrated the capacity to engage in self-learning and who cannot attend traditional institutions.

Every course has a syllabus or course outline that identifies the concepts or ideas considered to be significant to the particular course. It also contains a list of performance-based objectives that require the student to identify, define, explain, discuss, or summarize topics relevant to the course. Main texts for coursework are assigned, with the student utilizing the resources of local public or nearby school libraries. A student receives as much direction, guidance and assistance as required by his or her own unique program.

Experiential learning credit is awarded for previous work and life experience that is evaluated by faculty as it relates to the specific degree program.

NORTHWOOD UNIVERSITY

Contact:
Northwood University
Michigan Outreach Center
3225 Cook Road
Midland, Michigan 48640-2398

Telephone:
517-837-4411
Toll free: 800-445-5873
FAX: 517-832-9590

Degrees Offered: Associate of Arts (A.A.); Bachelor of Business Administration (B.B.A.) in Management or International Business

Summary: Business undergraduate degree program emphasizing a system of values in free-market enterprise activities; independent study program

Fees:
Application fee: $15
Work/Life Evaluation Assessment fee: $600
Correspondence Course Tuition (per credit hour): $185

Accreditation: North Central Association of Colleges and Schools

Residency: none

Narration:

Northwood University's mission is to prepare aspiring students of any age or station for a productive leadership career in an economic system of free markets and private enterprise. Northwood is a "values-driven" educational institution, differing from more traditional open inquiry institutions by preparing its graduates to be effective agents of private enterprise. Emanating from the Judeo-Christian tradition, which is characterized by respect for the family, individual work, faithfulness in personal relationships (including a respect for what belongs to others), truthfulness, and the notion of private property, the "Northwood Idea" includes the values of the work ethic, kindness, and responsibility toward the conditions of others.

The External Degree Program is geared to the student whose time or work schedule does not allow participation in traditional classes. A variety of course formats including independent study options are available to students. Directed study with concentrated, periodic instruction is also available.

Work experiences and other significant learning can be evaluated in terms of college credit by the Work/Life Evaluation process, permitting students by bypass course work for which they have already acquired equivalent college-level learning. This process evaluates seminars and workshops, military courses, community service, church activities, licenses and non-credit coursework. The college places no limits on the amount of learning it recognizes in equating college credit. However, 36 quarter hours of Northwood credit are required for a degree from Northwood University.

OHIO UNIVERSITY

Contact:
Ohio University
Adult Learning Services
301 Tupper Hall
Athens, Ohio 45701-2979

Telephone: 614-593-2150
Toll free: 800-444-2420

Degrees Offered: Associate in Arts (A.A.); Associate in Science (A.S.); Associate in Individualized Studies (A.I.S.); Associate of Applied Science in Security/Safety Technology (A.A.S.); Associate of Applied Business in Business Management Technology (A.A.B.); Certificate program in Business Management Technology; Bachelor of Specialized Studies (B.S.S.)

Summary: Correspondence courses and flexible undergraduate degree programs that may be built around individual career interests; many options exist for earning college credit for previous life experiences

Fees:
Application and evaluation: $100
Independent Study through Correspondence (per quarter hour): $50 plus $10 per course fee
Course Credit by Examination (per credit hour): $27
Independent Study projects (per quarter hour): $57

Accreditation: North Central Association of Colleges and Schools

Residency: none

Narration:

Several options for earning degree credit are available. Independent Study through Correspondence provides students with study guides and supplementary study aids with which to complete correspondence courses. Faculty members assist students through the program. Course Credit by Examination offers the opportunity for students to earn credit by taking a comprehensive examination. The Independent Study Projects option allows students to contract for a course that is not regularly offered through correspondence or examination. Credit for Prior Learning is a program that allows up to one full year of college credit to be earned through evaluation of past work or life experiences. To obtain prior learning credit, students must enroll in the life and career experiences course. Credit also may be given for noncollegiate training.

The Bachelor of Specialized Studies degree provides students the opportunity to design an individual degree plan. Similarly, the Associate in Individualized Studies degree is a self-designed degree program in which the student submits a proposed course of study with one area of concentration.

OKLAHOMA CITY UNIVERSITY

Contact:
Oklahoma City University
Petree College of Arts and Sciences
2501 N. Blackwelder
Oklahoma City, OK 73106

Telephone:
405-521-5265
Toll free: 800-633-7242

Degrees Offered: Bachelor of Arts (B.A.) in Liberal Arts; Bachelor of Science (B.S.) in Computer Science (additional majors offered through other divisions of the university)

Summary: Highly individualized system for granting college credit and undergraduate degrees for previous life and work experience, independent study classes or directed reading

Fees:
Evaluation fee: $15

Accreditation: North Central Association of Colleges and Schools

Residency:

Narration:
The Competency Based Degree Program is designed to meet the specific needs and busy schedules of working adults. It is a non-traditional program that allows a student to earn an undergraduate degree by granting university course credit for prior knowledge, helping the student attain needed credits without spending hours in the classroom. The student must have a tentative evaluation before entering the program. A wide range of activities are considered for college credit: several types of college entrance exams, United States Armed Forces tests, various banking tests, Federal Aviation licenses and courses, technical or trade school courses and other home study classes.

A student may achieve credit through independent study and directed readings as well as experiential learning. The student and the program coordinator will determine the areas of study needed and how best to fulfill degree requirements.

ORAL ROBERTS UNIVERSITY

Contact:
Oral Roberts University
School of LifeLong Education
7777 South Lewis Avenue
Tulsa, Oklahoma 74171

Telephone: 918-495-6236
Toll free: 800-678-8876

Degrees Offered: Bachelor of Science (B.S.) in Business Administration, Christian Care and Counseling, Church Ministries, and

93

Elementary Christian School Education

Summary: Christian university offering non-residential under-graduate degrees that transmit the ethos and spirit of the church.

Fees:
Application fee: $25
Tuition (per credit hour): $100

Accreditation: North Central Association of Colleges and Schools

Residency: none

Narration:
It is the purpose of Oral Roberts University, in its commitment to the historic Christian faith, to assist the student in his or her quest for knowledge of their relationship to God, man, and the universe. The Code of Honor is the central criterion of conduct for all who are a part of the University community. It is a concept of personal honor based on the principles of integrity, common sense, reverence for God, esteem for humankind, and respect for social and spiritual laws. When students enroll, they voluntarily accept a unique way of life that seeks to provide development of the spirit and body on the same high level as that of the intellect.

The External Degree program incorporates printed materials in the form of Study Guides and textbooks supplemented by other teaching aids as well as communication with a course instructor. This method of study allows the student to study at home. Each course is constructed around three written assignments and a final exam. The student may select a proctor who is a practicing professional to monitor exams. Courses may be taken at any time during the year. Students have four months from the date of enrollment to complete courses. Students must take at least 12 semester hours in residency during the degree program process. This may be done during the summer months by attending on-campus modular courses.

College credit may be earned for prior learning by taking standardized examinations. The Prior Learning Assessment process recognizes the knowledge that adult learners have gained through non-college courses, on-the-job training, or personal study. Credit may be granted for knowledge acquired which is the equivalent knowledge taught in a specific course. Students document such knowledge by enrolling in a portfolio development course.

PENNSYLVANIA STATE UNIVERSITY

Contact:
Independent Learning
The Pennsylvania State University
128 Mitchell Building
University Park, Pennsylvania 16802-3693

Telephone:
814-865-5403
Toll free: 800-252-3592 (Pennsylvania residents)
800-458-3617 (Nationwide)
Bitnet: km15@PSUADMIN
Internet: klm5@OAS.PSU.EDU

Degrees Offered: Associate degrees in Business Administration, Dietetic Food Systems Management, and Letters, Arts, and Sciences; over 200 credit courses and 90 noncredit courses offered

Summary: Correspondence courses in a wide range of subjects; associate undergraduate degree programs

Fees:
Tuition (per credit hour): $98
Rental fees for course videos may apply

Accreditation: Middle States Association of Colleges and Schools

Narration:
Penn State offers a wide range of correspondence courses in Agriculture, Business, Earth and Mineral Sciences, Education, Engineering, Health and Human Development, Hotel and Restau-

rant Management, in addition to a variety of liberal arts and sciences offerings. The credits earned through these courses may be applied to baccalaureate and associate degree programs. Penn State offers courses to meet the requirements of three extended associate degrees and several certificate programs. Independent Learning makes its college credit courses available to gifted high school seniors.

A correspondence course usually consists of a study guide and a textbook, but sometimes additional reference books, supplies, or other media (video and/or audio cassettes or televised lessons) may be required.

A student may register for an Independent Learning course at any time, but work from any previous course must be completed before enrolling in a new one. However, in a degree program a student may register for up to three Independent Learning courses simultaneously with the permission of the dean of the appropriate college. Degree and provisional students must complete a course in six months; extended degree students have one year for completion. Examinations must be administered by a qualified proctor who is a member of an academic community that the student selects and approves with Penn State.

PRESCOTT COLLEGE

Contact:
Adult Degree Program
Prescott College
220 Grove Avenue
Prescott, Arizona 86301

Telephone: 602-776-7116

Degrees Offered: Bachelor of Arts (B.A.) in Teacher Education/Certification, Management, Human Services/Counseling, and Environmental Studies; Individualized Liberal Arts programs in Environmental Education, Environmental Studies, Holistic Health, Therapeutic Recreation, Women Studies, Art, Humanities, Natural History, Photography, Public Administration, Communications, Political Science, Ethnobotany, or AgroEcology; Master of Arts Program (M.A.P.)

Summary: Highly individualized degree programs

Fees:
Application fee: $25
Tuition (per credit hour): $150

Accreditation: North Central Association of Colleges and Schools

Residency: Limited; students must attend an orientation weekend prior to beginning their program, and a Liberal Arts Seminar

Narration:

The Adult Degree Program is designed to encourage student involvement in program planning. The program allows a student to individualize a degree plan to meet specific career or personal goals, and then work closely with an advisor to design the overall structure of their program. The most important component of the student program is the development of learning contracts. Students participate in determining the objectives and activities of their courses through writing a learning contract for each course. Finally, each program incorporates an individually designed internship or experiential component which demonstrates competence in the student's field.

The Master of Arts Program provides graduate students with a great deal of flexibility in designing their own study programs in the areas of counseling and psychology; cultural and regional studies; education; environmental studies; humanities; and outdoor education/wilderness leadership. Students are expected to design highly individual programs of study that are both interdisciplinary and multi-cultural. The majority of graduate students continue to hold jobs and have family responsibilities while they pursue their education.

Qualified students have the option of writing a life experience portfolio or enrolling in a practicum course to organize and articulate experiential learning for the purpose of earning credit.

QUEEN'S UNIVERSITY

Contact:
Part-Time Studies
Office of the Registrar
Queen's University
Kingston, Ontario
K7L 3N6 Canada

Telephone:
613-545-2218

Degrees Offered: Bachelor of Arts (B.A.) in German, Political Studies or Psychology (also English, History, Mathematics, Religious Studies, Sociology and Women's Studies if the student takes up to 7 courses through other universities and transfers credit to Queen's)

Summary: Non-resident correspondence courses (offered during the time period of the regular school term); optional seminars

Fees:
Application fee: $25
Tuition:
        Full Course: $405.20
        Half Course: $202.60
International Student Tuition Fees: Please write to the university for complete information.

Accreditation:

Residency: none

Narration:
        Correspondence study is designed for students who want to continue their formal education, but find it impossible to do so through regular class work on- or off-campus. Each correspondence course counts as a credit or half-credit toward a degree in the same way as the equivalent course given on campus. There is no limit to the number of correspondence courses that may be included in a degree program.
        The length of the courses is as follows: Fall Term, Septem-

ber to December; Fall-Winter Term, September to April; Winter Term, January to April; Spring-Summer Session, May to August. Half-credit courses are offered in Fall Term, Winter Term or Spring-Summer Session. Full-credit courses are offered in Fall-Winter Session or Spring-Summer Session. Courses have limited enrollments and fill up quickly.

One weekend seminar per term is offered in Kingston for most correspondence courses. These seminars provide an opportunity to meet with instructors, tutors and fellow students. Attendance at the seminars is not compulsory. Study skills and library workshops are held several times throughout the year for part-time students. Students may call their instructor or tutor collect to discuss course material.

REGENTS COLLEGE OF THE UNIVERSITY OF THE STATE OF NEW YORK

Contact:
Regents College
1450 Western Avenue
Albany, New York 12203-3524

Degrees Offered: 26 different degree programs at associate and baccalaureate levels in business, liberal arts, nursing, and technology, including: Associate in Arts (A.A.) in Liberal Arts; Associate in Science (A.S.) in Liberal Arts, Business, Computer Software, Electronics Technology, Nuclear Technology, Technology (with Specialty); Bachelor of Arts (B.A.) in Liberal Arts; Bachelor of Science (B.S.) in Computer Information Systems, Computer Technology, Electronics Technology, Nuclear Technology, and Technology (with Specialty); Associate in Applied Science (Nursing), Associate in Science (Nursing), and Bachelor of Science (Nursing).

Summary: Regents College is the external degree program of The University of the State of New York. No classes are offered, but degrees are granted with college credits earned by a variety of methods including examinations, courses from other institutions, and distance learning courses.

Fees:
Enrollment/Initial Evaluation Fee: $510
Annual Advisement and Evaluation Fee: $250
Credit Review Fee: $95

Accreditation: Middle States Association of Colleges and Schools; National League for Nursing

Residency: none

Narration:

Regents College is the external degree program of The University of the State of New York, and serves 15,000 students each year. The College does not teach courses; it advises the student on how to complete rigorous degree requirements through a variety of credit sources, including regular classroom courses at other institutions, correspondence courses, examinations, and military, business, and industry training. Faculty committees establish degree requirements, determine the ways in which credit can be earned, develop the content for all examinations, and review the records of students to verify their degree completion. Students in each program are required to demonstrate expertise in a field of specialization, either as preparation for graduate school or for entry into or advancement within a career or profession. Enrollments are accepted all year, and students may complete their degrees at their own pace.

DistanceLearn is a database of information on thousands of courses and examinations from regionally accredited colleges that are currently available at a distance. Some of these courses use technologies such as video, audio, or computer to deliver or enhance the course (in addition to print materials such as textbooks). Using the database, the academic advisor can conduct a search tailored to the student's needs and preferences, and send a printout of a few courses or exams appropriate to the student's degree program. The database also includes information on credit-by-examination programs, including Regents' Special Assessment program that offers an individualized examination on any college-level subject that cannot be adequately assessed through a standardized proficiency examination. Students who wish to locate other Regents College students in their own region or degree program to form study or learning support groups and to share information about local learning resources may join the Regents College Learning Network for a modest annual fee.

REGIS UNIVERSITY

Contact:
Regis University
School for Professional Studies
3333 Regis Blvd.
Denver, Colorado 80221-1099

Telephone:
Undergraduate:
    303-458-4300
    Toll free: 800-967-3237
Graduate:
    303-458-4080
    Toll free: 800-677-9270

Degrees Offered: Bachelor of Arts (B.A.)—Individualized degrees; Bachelor of Science in Business Administration (B.S.B.A.) offered in conjunction with Mind Extension University; Master of Arts in Liberal Studies (M.L.S.); teacher certification and counseling licensure programs

Summary: Jesuit tradition university with 14 regional campuses; affiliated with Mind Extension University (via cable and satellite)

Fees:
Tuition (per semester hour):
    Guided independent study: $240
    Televised courses offered through Mind Extension University: $165

Accreditation: North Central Association of Colleges and Schools

Residency: minimal; a registration and orientation program for new students.

Narration:

The Bachelor of Science Degree in Business Administration includes a minor in Social Science and is presented in an accelerated 8-week format (for every 3 credits). Courses for the degree program are cable and satellite delivered to over 23 million households nationwide through Mind Extension University. They are also available on videotape. The student chooses a combination of course work through the Regis University/Mind Extension University program and through a selection of other educational options. Throughout the degree program, the student remains in direct contact with an advisor, faculty and other students as they work together.

The Bachelor of Arts degree program is designed for adults seeking an individualized and flexible way to earn a degree. The key element in the Regis program is communication among students, advisors and course consultants or resource persons by telephone, fax, and mail. Faculty advisors work directly with students in developing individual degree plans. A student's degree plan may include guided independent study and research, televised courses, internships for learning on the job, workshops, seminars, lectures, and other appropriate methods of learning. Students may learn how to translate their own life learning into college credit through Assessment of Prior Learning.

The Regis University School for Professional Studies offers an individualized, self-designed master's degree. The Master of Arts Degree in Liberal Studies emphasizes the connection among disciplines and is distinguished by its ethical, global, and interdisciplinary emphases. Students may concentrate their work in any one of four areas: Education, Language and Communication, Psychology, or Social Science.

Students may acquire Colorado or Wyoming teacher certification in early childhood, elementary, middle school, secondary, English as a second language, or special education. This may be combined with a bachelor's degree, or done separately or combined with the Master of Arts in Liberal Studies if the student has already completed a bachelor's degree. The majority of course work will be completed through the campus-free, guided independent study format. However, student teaching must be done in Colorado or Wyoming, as appropriate. Students in the Master of Arts in Liberal Studies may select the Licensed Professional Counselor track, entailing 48 semester hours of graduate work prior to sitting for the examination, plus a 2,000 hour internship.

Regis offers credit for documented learning from actual work/life experiences through Portfolio Assessment.

RENSSELAER POLYTECHNIC INSTITUTE

Contact:
Rensselaer Satellite Video Program
Office of Continuing Education
CII Suite 4011
Rensselaer Polytechnic Institute
Troy, New York 12180-3590

Telephone:
518-276-RSVP (276-7787)
FAX: 518-276-8026

Degrees Offered: Master of Science (M.S.) in Manufacturing Systems Engineering, Management of Technology, Microelectronics Manufacturing, Mechanical Engineering, Computer Science, or Technical Communication. Certificate programs are available in Computer Science, Management of Technology, Manufacturing Systems, Mechanical Engineering, Microelectronics Manufacturing, Reliability, Information Science, Robotics and Automation, and Technical Communication. Non-matriculated courses are also available.

Summary: Graduate degree programs for corporate delivery using satellite, videotape, and/or interactive compressed video technology

Fees:
Tuition (per 3-credit course): $1,515

Accreditation: Accreditation Board for Engineering and Technology

Residency: Courses delivered on-site at corporations

Narration:

The Rensselaer Satellite Video Program offers businesses, industries and government agencies state-of-the-art distance learning technology. Students remain at their worksites learning the same material and earning the same advanced degrees as resident graduate students. Site Coordinators receive and distribute instructional materials which regularly include: textbooks, syllabi, course schedules, class notes/handouts, and examinations. Site Coordinators also assist in the exchange of homework. Assignments are mailed to the sites, distributed according to local procedures, and upon completion are returned to Rensselaer using express delivery services.

Rensselaer students are encouraged to communicate regularly with the staff who will respond to questions concerning curricular requirements, course content, and individual academic needs. The video network is used to provide regular "live" office hours with faculty to answer questions, respond to comments, and provide guidance to students. An important aspect of the academic advising process is submission of a required Plan of Study, which establishes the route each student will travel in pursuit of a degree.

An on-site tape library is available that is comprised of lectures broadcast during the current semester. Program students can review instruction as often as they wish, and some sites allow students to check out tapes for home viewing.

The Computer Science department has strong links with industry. Faculty and students are regularly engaged in contracts sponsored by major corporations. The industry/education partnership is particularly important with regard to academic computing. Certain graduate courses and curricula available through Rensselaer are computer intensive, and employers must ensure that participants can access required hardware and software detailed in course descriptions.

The Management of Technology graduate program was specifically designed to address the needs of middle and upper level engineers and scientists who find themselves in positions of leadership. It provides a synthesis of the principles of management and technology necessary for strategic leadership in a modern technological environment.

ROGER WILLIAMS COLLEGE

Contact:
Roger Williams College
School of Continuing Education
Bristol, Rhode Island 02809

Telephone:
401-253-1990

Degrees Offered: Associate in Arts (A.A.), Associate in Science (A.S.), Bachelor of Arts (B.A.), Bachelor of Fine Arts (B.F.A.) in Creative Writing, Bachelor of Science (B.S.) offered through Continuing Education with a minimum of campus-located instruction.

Students who are geographically removed from the campus may enroll in the following bachelor's degree programs: Administration of Justice, Business Administration, Historic Preservation, Industrial Technology, or Public Administration if they are able to enter as juniors or seniors.

Summary: Minimal residency and long-distance degree programs; many options for receiving college credit for previous life/work experience

Fees:
Application fee: $35
Tuition:
Comprehensive Full Open Program Rate:
3 credit hours: $1,170; 6 credit hours: $2,340; 9 credit hours: $3,510; 12 credit hours: $4,680; 15 credit hours: $5,820

Other Than Regular Open Program Comprehensive Rate—
3 credit hours: $375; 6 credit hours: $750; 9 credit hours: $1,125; 12 credit hours: $4,680; 15 credit hours: $5,820

Residency: Limited; some long-distance learning programs available

Narration:

The Open Program of the School of Continuing Education is a comprehensive external degree program. It offers individualized education for working adults, making them able to pursue educational programs with little or no interference with their personal, family, or job commitments. Either full-time or part-time study is available. It is a time-shortened degree program because of the academic credit awarded for past job experience, relevant life experiences, personal enrichment activities, prior college attendance, military training and experience, and examinations. It also offers selected programs to students who are geographically removed from the main campus and who are unable to be in residence. The Open Program emphasizes the availability of self-directed study and offers continuous advisement throughout the year. It establishes a working relationship between each student and a personal faculty advisor.

Students may be granted advanced credit toward their degree through the following: up to two years of credit may be granted for past life and work experience, personal enrichment, or participation in conferences and workshops. Up to three years of credit may be granted for military training and/or experience. Up to two years of credit may be granted for exams that measure the learning of an individual compared with a student who has completed two years of college. A wide variety of subjects can be tested.

SAYBROOK INSTITUTE

Contact:
Saybrook Institute
1550 Sutter Street
San Francisco, California 94109

Telephone:
415-441-5034

Degrees Offered: Master of Arts (M.A.) programs in Psychology or Human Science; Doctor of Philosophy (Ph.D.) in Psychology or Human Science

Summary: Humanistic psychology graduate programs that encourage research; innovative, individualized distance learning

Fees:
Student fee: $50
Tuition (annual): $9,000

Accreditation: Western Association of Schools and Colleges

Residency: Limited; students are required to attend two five-day Residential Conferences each year

Narration:

The mission of the Institute is to provide a unique and creative environment for graduate study, research, and communication in humanistic psychology and human science, focused on understanding and enhancing the human experience. A distinctive aspect of Saybrook is its mode of education, a dispersed education format. This is an adaptation of the European tutorial model which emphasizes a one-to-one interaction between students and faculty. Using learning guides, students complete coursework in guided independent study. Their progress and performance are encouraged and evaluated by faculty who communicate in person or by phone, letter, or computer. While much of the student's intellectual work is done independently, the relationship between faculty and student provides for commentary and analysis that is equivalent to what occurs in traditional classroom situations.

The primary instructional materials used by students are learning guides, which have been specially prepared by the faculty for each course. These guides outline the expectations of the course and the required reading and writing assignments. To supplement the instructional program available through the Institute, students are expected to make use of resources in their communities such as public and university libraries, courses at other graduate schools, in-service training programs, and private tutors.

SKIDMORE COLLEGE

Contact:
Skidmore College
University without Walls
Saratoga Springs, New York 12866-1632

Telephone:
518-584-5000, ext. 2295

Degrees Offered: Bachelor of Arts, Bachelor of Science

Summary: Flexible undergraduate degree-granting program; credit granted for a variety of activities including guided independent study; no formal classes offered

Fees:
Application fee: $30
Enrollment fee (annual 12-month period): $1,850
Independent study with Skidmore faculty member: $250
Evaluation of a self-directed study: $50
Final project assessment (three assessors each receive $50): $150

Accreditation: Middle States Association of Colleges and Schools

Residency: Limited; students are required to attend three on-campus meetings

Narration:
University without Walls does not offer courses; it confers degrees that are earned in a variety of ways. A student can use educational resources available wherever he/she lives—the local community college or university, or other resources for learning such as jobs, internships, directed independent study, or courses offered at a distance by major universities. Others will choose to work more independently, with faculty from local colleges or from Skidmore, in courses designed specifically for their needs. Some will choose to learn in very non-traditional environments—an archaeological dig in Central America, a shelter for battered women, a Head Start classroom. Most students will find exciting ways to combine different styles of learning into an individualized

education. What makes this diversity possible is the unique advising system, where each student plays a major role in shaping a plan of study that is rigorous, challenging and able to be achieved within the realities of his/her own life.

Students may apply, begin their programs, or complete their degree requirements at any time during the year. Students are required to attend three on-campus meetings: the admissions interview; the first advising sessions at which the student's program is initiated; and the degree plan meeting at which the student's program is formally reviewed by the standing committee of faculty.

Each plan of individualized study provides a broad base in the liberal arts as well as an area of focus that allows the student to specialize: whether in a traditional field, a preprofessional field, or an independently designed, interdisciplinary program that does not fit traditional categories.

SOUTHEASTERN COLLEGE OF THE ASSEMBLIES OF GOD

Contact:
Southeastern College of the Assemblies of God
Continuing Education Department
1000 Longfellow Blvd.
Lakeland, Florida 33801-6099

Telephone:
813-665-4404
FAX: 813-666-8103

Degrees Offered: Bachelor of Arts (B.A.) in Bible, Christian Education, Bible and Missions, or Bible and Practical Ministry

Summary: Non-resident undergraduate degrees in Christian topics

Fees:
Application fee: $35
Orientation/counseling fee: $50
Enrollment fee: $50

Portfolio Evaluation of prior experiential learning (per credit hour): $60
Independent Studies tuition (per credit hour): $60
Faculty Exams (per credit hour): $60

Accreditation: Southern Association of Colleges and Schools

Residency: none

Narration:

The External Degree Program provides students an alternative approach to the undergraduate educational experience. The program provides the opportunity for personal or professional development as related to Biblical, ministerial, and theological studies utilizing the independent study method whereby courses are provided by the college and completed by the student at his/her place of residency. Several students may enroll for an Independent Study course and engage a local educator or pastor to serve as the class coordinator. Prior experiential learning also may be evaluated for college credit.

SOUTHEASTERN UNIVERSITY

Contact:
Southeastern University
501 Eye Street, S.W.
Washington, D.C. 20024

Telephone:
202-488-8162
FAX: 202-488-8093

Degrees Offered: Associate of Science (A.S.) in General Studies, Business Management or Accounting; Bachelor of Science (B.S.) in General Studies, Business Management or Accounting; Master of Business Administration (M.B.A.)

Summary: Undergraduate degrees in business through distance learning; limited residency

Fees:
Registration fee (per term): $125
Tuition (per credit hour): $142
Residency requirement tuition and registration fee (9 credits): $1,403
Work/Life Learning (per 3 credits): $426
Challenge Examination: $426
Transcript Evaluation: $25

Accreditation: Middle States Association of Colleges and Schools

Residency: Limited; two weeks of intensive residencies required

Narration:
      The Distance Learning Degree Program is a non-traditional program offering undergraduate and graduate career education in business management and accounting. Through individual, guided study, the student learns in personal surroundings with the flexibility of home study. The educational system of guided, individualized study is quite different from traditional on-campus learning. The "teacher" is not a single individual as in a college classroom, but rather a composite of researchers, authors, instructors, testing specialists, and leading practitioners in accounting, business administration, and the liberal arts who collaborate on the units studied. Each student receives the personal attention and assistance his/her individual needs demand. The intructional materials are written by recognized professionals who are actively engaged in the very work they are writing about. This makes the educational materials realistic, contemporary, and authoritative, providing the student with practical, as well as theoretical, knowledge. In addition to studying the instructional material, the student will interact with the faculty through testing, correspondence, telecommunications, and direct instruction in residencies. The special projects and examinations that are submitted by the student will be individually corrected, evaluated, and graded to assure maximum comprehension of the subjects.
      College credit may be earned through the academic assessment of prior college level learning acquired through life or work roles or through selected educational programs offered by noncol-

legiate organizations. Experience is applied on a course-by-course basis when it appears that learning resulting from experiences is compatible with the learning content of specific courses. Credit may also be obtained through successful performance on a proficiency examination; students are limited to 9 credit hours by examination.

SOUTHWESTERN ADVENTIST COLLEGE

Contact:
Adult Degree Program
Southwestern Adventist College
Keene, Texas 76059

Telephone:
817-556-4705
Toll free: 800-433-2240
FAX: 817-556-4742

Degrees Offered: Associate of Science (A.S.), Bachelor of Arts (B.A.), Bachelor of Science (B.S.), Bachelor of Business Administration (B.B.A.), teacher certification. Majors include communication, Education, English, Office Administration, Office Information Systems, Psychology, Religion, and Social Science.

Summary: Seventh-Day Adventist college offering undergraduate degrees through independent study; credit granted for life experiences through examinations and portfolio assessment

Fees:
Tuition (12 hour package @ $233 per hour): $2,796
(6 hour package @ $233 per hour): $1,398
Seminar fee: $75
Recording fees for experiential credit (for each class, 1 to 4 hours): $20.

Accreditation: Southern Association of Colleges and Schools

Residency: Limited; one-week seminar

Narration:

The Adult Degree Program enables a student to acquire college credit through a variety of means. Proficiency exams allow a student to demonstrate college-level knowledge in a given subject area. Students may have prior learning from work and other experiences that may be assessed for college credit by means of a portfolio, a document assembled by the student for the faculty to review. Non-collegiate courses and seminars may also be counted for college credit. Independent study by mail, telephone, and other technologies is the primary way of taking college classes without residency on campus.

For independent study, the instructor gives the student a basic syllabus for the class and discusses the appropriate method of study. The instructor will monitor the student's progress through letters, phone calls, cassettes, quizzes, tests, reports, research papers, and final exams.

SOUTHWESTERN ASSEMBLIES OF GOD COLLEGE

Contact:
Southwestern Assemblies of God College
Division of Adult and Continuing Education
1200 Sycamore
Waxahachie, Texas 75165

Telephone:
214-937-4010
toll free: 800-262-7242

Degrees Offered: Bachelor of Career Arts (B.C.A.), Biblical Studies Diploma (B.S.D.)

Summary: Bible-based undergraduate degree program offered through short residencies and distance study

Fees:
Application fee: $30
Tuition (per semester hour): $110
General fee

1-8 hours (per semester hour): $14
9 or more hours: $130
Experiential learning credit portfolio assessment fee: $150

Accreditation: Southern Association of Colleges and Schools

Residency: Limited; one-week introductory seminar required and two-day Progress Seminars every semester

Narration:

The Division of Adult and Continuing Education provides a traditional Bible-based educational experience through an innovative, non-traditional format. Students attend a week-long introductory seminar on campus where faculty members assist the student in designing a personal degree plan, and then attend two-day progress seminars each semester. Each course syllabus is structured to provide step-by-step assistance through the assignments. Exams that require supervision are administered through a designated local individual. Many assignments and projects are designed to take advantage of one's particular work situation, thus increasing the quality of a person's learning experiences. The student may contact the professor toll-free at any time during a course.

Majors are offered in Business, Church Ministries, Professional Studies, Interdisciplinary Studies for Elementary Teachers, and Biblical Studies.

SAINT JOSEPH'S COLLEGE

Contact:
Saint Joseph's College
External Degree Programs
Windham, Maine 04062-1198

Telephone:
207-892-6766
Toll free: 800-343-5498

Degrees Offered: Associate of Science in Management (A.S.), Bachelor of Science in Health Care Administration (B.S.H.C.A.); Bachelor of Science in Business Administration (B.S.B.A); Bachelor of Science in Professional Arts (B.S.P.A.), Bachelor of Science in Radiologic Technology (B.S.R.T.). Master in Health Services Administration. Certificate programs in Health Care Management, or Business Administration

Summary: Catholic college offering degrees in health care fields and business; short summer session residency requirement

Fees:
Application fee: $50
Certificate Programs Application Fee: $25
Tuition (minimum of two courses, 6 semester hour credits at $150 per credit): $900
Portfolio fee: $125

Accreditation: New England Association of Schools and Colleges

Residency: Limited; some summer residency sessions required

Narration:
Founded in 1912 by the Sisters of Mercy, Saint Joseph's is an institution which in its teachings professes fidelity to the Gospel and to the doctrines and heritage of the Roman Catholic Church. It offers adult learners the opportunity to integrate formal education in the liberal arts tradition with professional experience. The External Degree Program provides academic options such as individualized programs of study and personalized instruction through faculty-directed independent study. The College integrates its faculty-directed study structure with an opportunity to meet and learn with peers in a required two-week summer residency program.

There are many options for earning credit from degree-related job experiences, including hospital-based education programs, certificate programs, and other related professional programs. In addition, undergraduate degree entrants may submit a portfolio demonstrating experiential learning for possible credit.

Within the Master in Health Services Administration Program, the student pursues all course work when and where the student chooses. At the same time, an on-campus Academic Advisor monitors the student's progress and serves as a link with faculty. Up to six credits may be awarded for experiential learning through submission of an experiential learning portfolio. There is a required two-week campus residency held during the summer.

SAINT MARY-OF-THE-WOODS COLLEGE

Contact:
Saint Mary-of-the-Woods College
Women's External Degree Program
Saint Mary-of-the-Woods, Indiana 47876-0070

Telephone:
812-535-5106
Toll free: 800-926-SMWC (926-7692)

Degrees Offered: Baccalaureate degrees in Accounting, Business Administration, Education, English, Equine Studies, History/Political Science, Humanities, Journalism, Marketing, Management, Paralegal Studies, Psychology, Social Science, Social Work, and Theology. Associate majors are General Business, Gerontology, Humanities, and Paralegal Studies. Certificates available in Gerontology, Paralegal Studies, and Theology

Summary: Catholic college offering undergraduate and certificate degrees especially designed to fit women's lives and schedules

Fees:
Application fee: $35
Tuition (per credit hour): $195
Life Experience Credit (per hour): $77

Accreditation: North Central Association of Colleges and Schools

Residency: Limited; students come to campus once each semester

Narration:

116

Saint Mary-of-the-Woods is a Catholic college dedicated to educating women personally and professionally while continuing family and job responsibilities. The Women's External Degree Program allows students to earn college degrees in a guided, independent study format at their residence, coming to campus each semester to plan and register for courses. Using course outlines that specify learning activities and outcomes, the student and instructor plan the semester. Throughout the semester, regular contact is maintained between student and instructor by mail, phone, tapes, or computer modem.

Students have the option of earning credits by means of Life Experience Credit applications, where credit awards are made on the basis of college-level knowledge gained through employment, volunteer work, non-college based training programs, or other means.

STATE UNIVERSITY SYSTEM OF FLORIDA

Contact:
State University System of Florida
External Degree Program
University of South Florida
Tampa, Florida 33620-8400

Telephone:
813-974-4058
Toll free: 800-635-1484

Degrees Offered: Bachelor of Independent Studies (B.I.S.)

Summary: Limited-residency interdisciplinary degree undergraduate program

Fees:
Admission fee: $15
Tuition (assessed in blocks of 15 semester hours for a tutorial, seminar or thesis planning)
In-state ($40.36 per credit hour):
Out-of-state ($132.33 per credit hour)

Accreditation: Southern Association of Colleges and Schools

Residency: Limited; short-term summer sessions

Narration:

The External Degree Program is designed for adults who find it difficult to attend regular university classes because of career or family commitments. The student proceeds at his/her own pace and location, except for periodic, short-term summer sessions.

The Bachelor of Independent Studies program is available through participating state universities: Florida State University, the University of Florida, the University of North Florida, and the University of South Florida. The three major learning strategies of this program are guided independent study (the tutorial), residential seminars, and a senior or interarea thesis. The tutorial is essentially print intensive. The student reads and interacts with a faculty advisor until such time as the advisor indicates that the student is prepared to sit for the area comprehensive examination. Tutorials are completed in between 6 and 24 months, and are followed by a comprehensive exam in order to demonstrate that a satisfactory level of proficiency has been attained in the independent study component of a particular area. The exam may be taken on- or off-campus.

The program is based on a curriculum of interdisciplinary studies as opposed to concentration in a particular field. Representing multiple disciplines, the curriculum is divided into four study areas—Social Sciences, Natural Sciences, Humanities, and Interarea Studies. Students may apply for a waiver of up to two areas of guided independent study by demonstrating their level of competence by means of exams. However, most applicants with prior learning utilize the abbreviated reading program. In this instance the student bypasses the area disciplines in which he or she is competent and is directed to read in the others in order to receive credit.

STEPHENS COLLEGE

Contact:
Stephens College Without Walls
Campus Box 2083
Columbia, Missouri 65215

Telephone: 314-876-7125
Toll free: 800-388-7579

Degrees Offered: Bachelor of Arts (B.A.) in Business Administration; Philosophy, Law and Rhetoric; Health Science or Health Care, Psychology, or English. Bachelor of Science (B.S.) in Health Information Management or Early Childhood Education

Summary: Independent study and external degree program for both men and women

Fees:
Application fee: $50
First year program tuition (3 courses with Stephens faculty): $1,875
Annual program tuition (2 courses with Stephens faculty): $1,250
Preadvising: $150
Prior learning portfolio evaluation (1 to 3 credit hour courses): $625
　　　Each additional 1 credit hour course: $225
Management program courses: $400

Accreditation: North Central Association of Colleges and Schools

Residency: Limited; must begin program by taking Liberal Studies Seminar on campus (offered seven times a year for five days or two weekends)

Narration:
　　　The External Degree Program is designed to complement the student's commitments to work, family and community. Working with faculty members, students in the program study at home. Faculty provide students with a syllabus, assignments, readings and the names of required textbooks. Students have six months in which to complete a course; with faculty permission an additional six months may be granted. Each student plans an

individual program of study with the help of an advisor.

Students with unique learning objectives can establish contract courses to be fulfilled through independent study. A faculty member is assigned to work with a student to design a course, determine objectives and content, texts, method of evaluation, amount of credit and level of the course.

Students may prepare portfolios for the assessment of prior learning. Prior learning is based on the premise that significant learning can be acquired through knowledge and experience and that adult students should be recognized for college-level learning which can be successfully documented through a portfolio-writing process. Credit is not awarded for the experience itself, but rather for the knowledge of theory which the student has obtained as a result of the experience. No letter grades are given. College credit may also be obtained through the assessment of college-level learning in noncollegiate, accredited, professional training programs. Standardized examinations for course credit may be taken in English, humanities, mathematics, natural science and social sciences/history.

SUMMIT UNIVERSITY OF LOUISIANA

Contact:
Summit University of Louisiana
7508 Hayne Boulevard
New Orleans, Louisiana 70126

Telephone:
504-241-0227

Degrees Offered: Associate of Arts (A.A.) degree for life learning; Bachelor of Arts (B.A.), Bachelor of Science (B.S.), Master of Arts (M.A.), Master of Science (M.S.), Doctor of Philosophy (Ph.D.)

Summary: Assessment university; academic credit granted for lifelong learning, education obtained with tutors or from other educational institutions; no classes offered

Fees:

Total fee for A.A. degree for life learning: $96
All other degree programs (per 8-month academic year): $3,000
($1,500 per semester)

Accreditation: none

Residency: none

Narration:

      Summit is an assessment university that evaluates an individual's lifelong learning at B.A., M.A., and Ph.D. levels. Summit enrolls learners for a minimum of one academic year for B.A.s and M.A.s, and three semesters for the Ph.D. Summit assesses documented learning, confirms the design and scope of degrees, and determines how credits are to be evaluated and measured. The university assesses a wide range of degree programs adults have designed by combining significant life learning, independent studies and studies with personally contracted faculty, tutors, or learning institutions. Degree programs are in a specific area of personal interest that is uniquely the individual's, meeting life, career and academic goals. Summit does not offer instruction or courses and does not contract with community resources or faculty.

SYRACUSE UNIVERSITY

Contact:
Syracuse University
Independent Study Degree Programs
610 East Fayette Street
Syracuse, New York 13244-6020

Telephone:
315-443-ISDP (4737)
315-443-3284
FAX: 315-443-1928

Degrees: Associate of Arts (A.A.), Bachelor of Arts (B.A.) in Liberal

121

Studies, Bachelor of Science (B.S.) in Business Administration, Criminal Justice, Restaurant and Food-Service Management; Master of Business Administration (M.B.A.); Master of Library Science (M.L.S.); Master of Science in Nursing (M.S. in Nursing); Master of Social Science (M.S.Sc.); and Master of Arts (M.A.) with emphasis in either advertising design or illustration.

Summary: Limited-residency undergraduate and graduate degree programs; independent study format

Fees:
Application fee: $40
Undergraduate tuition (per credit hour): $262
Graduate tuition (per credit hour): $432
Advanced credit exams (per exam): $90

Accreditation: Middle States Association of Colleges and Secondary Schools; National League for Nursing

Residency: Limited; short, on-campus residency sessions

Narration:
　　　　Each of the independent study degree programs combines two elements: short on-campus residencies and self-paced study that the student completes at home. The required residency sets the pattern for the work the student does independently. The student is supplied with textbooks, article reprints, science kits, study guides, syllabi, and reading lists. Assignments are returned for evaluation by mail, fax, or e-mail. The student returns to campus at the end of the home study period for a day of wrap-up sessions or exams before beginning the next semester's week of classes. This program provides more flexibility than adult education classes that require attendance once or twice a week.

　　　　Syracuse's individual schools and colleges may assess and award credit for educational accomplishment attained in extra-institutional settings, including non-collegiate sponsors such as the military. Credit may be awarded for experience-based learning when such learning can be assigned to an academic discipline. Decisions on the experience-based credit award are based on an evaluation which usually takes place following the student's first semester of residency. Syracuse does not award graduate-level credit for professional experience.

THOMAS EDISON STATE COLLEGE

Contact:
Thomas Edison State College
101 W. State St.
Trenton, New Jersey 08608-1176

Telephone:
609-984-1150
FAX: 609-984-8447

Degrees Offered: Associate in Arts (A.A.); Associate in Applied Science in Radiologic Technology; Associate in Science (A.S.) in Management, Natural Sciences and Mathematics, Public and Social Services, or Applied Science and Technology; Bachelor of Arts (B.A.); Bachelor of Science in Business Administration, Applied Science and Technology, Human Services, or Nursing.

Summary: Non-residency undergraduate degree programs; flexible options for earning college credit

Fees:

	NJ resident	Nonresident
Application fee	$ 75	$ 75
Annual enrollment fee	$400	$400
Credit transfer evaluation fee		
Semester hours:		
1-5	$ 31	$ 62
6-11	$ 62	$124
12-29	$108	$216
30-59	$194	$388
60-89	$280	$560
90-120	$366	$732
Portfolio/Practicum,		
per credit attempted	$ 12	$ 18

Guided Study tuition,		
per credit attempted	$ 46	$ 69

Accreditation: Middle States Association of Colleges and Schools; National League for Nursing

Residency: none

Narration:

Thomas Edison State College is an undergraduate institution offering associate and baccalaureate degrees. The College primarily serves self-directed adult learners who have generally acquired or are acquiring college-level learning in noncollegiate settings and/or in previous college courses. The College offers no classroom instruction, has no residency requirement and has no full-time teaching faculty of its own. Students meet degree requirements by passing college equivalency examinations, assessment of college-level learning, the transfer of credits earned at other colleges and universities. There is no limit to the number of transfer credits accepted. Students also fulfill degree requirements by completing a variety of independent learning courses (audio, video, computer-facilitated). A student may enroll at any time and graduate as degree requirements are fulfilled.

The majority of students are able to earn credit through various assessment methods for prior learning. Through this process, the skills and knowledge students have acquired from their work experience, volunteer activities, training programs, hobbies, religious activities, homemaking skills, independent reading and special accomplishments can often be translated into college credit. These prior learning experiences include competencies developed through jobs, professions or careers; through previous noncollegiate post-secondary education; through formal learning experiences acquired in business, labor, military and leisure activities; and through special credentials.

The College offers more than 400 examinations for evaluating students' prior knowledge. All of the examinations reflect content areas that are commonly covered in courses that are taught in college classrooms. Credit is also granted for satisfactory performance on a number of standardized examinations. The College will grant credit for current professional licenses or certificates that have been evaluated and approved.

TRINITY UNIVERSITY

Contact:
Trinity University
Non-Traditional Graduate Programs in Health Care Administration
715 Stadium Drive
San Antonio, Texas 78212

Telephone:
210-736-8107

Degrees Offered: Certificate in Basic Health Care Administration, Master's Program in Health Care Administration

Summary: Non-traditional, practice-based external certification and master's degree programs in health care administration

Fees:
Application fee: $25
Tuition
      Certificate program (per course): $375
      Master's Program
        (per hour for students taking fewer than 12 semester hours): $482.50

Accreditation: Accrediting Commission on Education for Health Services Administration

Residency: Limited; each semester begins with a two- to three-day on-campus intensive instructional session followed by a five-month individual study period at home

Narration:
      The Department of Health Care Administration offers practice-based external certification and degree programs for working health care managers. These programs are designed for health care professionals desiring further education and certification, but whose responsibilities prevent them from attending traditional on-campus classes. The required residency for these programs is 2-3 days at the beginning of each semester. There are

five teleconference calls during the semester of 2 hours duration; assignments are mailed or faxed in during the semester.

The Certificate Program in Health Care Administration is designed for men and women who hold current management responsibilities in hospitals or other health care settings. This non-credit course of study leads to a Certificate in Basic Health Care Administration.

The Master's Program is an accredited executive program leading to a Master of Science in Health Care Administration. This program allows individuals currently employed in a health care setting to pursue work toward a graduate degree through courses completed independently by the participant under the supervision of an instructor. This non-traditional program is augmented by a unique teleconferencing network (which has the capacity to join all students in a class with an instructor through a telephone system) and computer-based assignments.

Trinity offers Individual Study Programs leading to the Certificate and Master's Degree that focus on the essential principles of health care administration by using the richness of the already established managerial experience of each participant. Since participants in the program must be currently employed in a managerial position in a health care setting, the principles of health care administration will be directly related to each student's particular experiences in health care management.

TROY STATE UNIVERSITY IN MONTGOMERY

Contact:
Troy State University in Montgomery
P.O. Drawer 4419
Montgomery, Alabama 36103-4419

Telephone:
205-834-1400

Degrees Offered: Associate of Science (A.S.) in General Studies, Bachelor of Arts (B.A.) in Professional Studies, Bachelor of Science (B.S.) in Professional Studies

Summary: Flexible undergraduate degree programs; credit may be earned through a variety of nontraditional means

Fees:
Tuition (per credit hour)
Contract courses, Alabama residents: $46
Contract courses, non-residents: $66
Annual participation fee: $100

Accreditation: Southern Association of Colleges and Schools

Residency: Limited; students must be present on campus for one day to defend their senior project

Narration:
The External Degree Program is specifically designed to provide quality educational opportunities to mature students who are unable to undertake studies in a traditional degree program because of work schedule, handicap, family, or geographical restrictions. A student can meet degree requirements by combining regular coursework with credit earned by nontraditional means: transfer of credit, television coursework or correspondence credits, evaluation of prior experiential learning through portfolio assessment, evaluation of previous military, business, or industry training, assessment of non-college learning through examinations, or independent study through learning contracts from Troy State.

Major areas of study for the Associate of Science in General Education degree are: Business Administration, Child Care, History, Political Science, Psychology, or Social Science. Major areas for the Bachelor of Arts/Science in Professional Studies are: English, History, Political Science, Psychology, Resource Management, and Social Science.

THE UNIVERSITY OF ALABAMA

Contact:
The University of Alabama

External Degree Program
P.O. Box 870182
Tuscaloosa, Alabama 35487-0182

Telephone:
205/348-6000

Degrees Offered: Bachelor of Arts (B.A.), Bachelor of Science (B.S.)

Summary: Undergraduate degrees and graduate classes in a wide variety of disciplines. Credit may be given for on-campus courses, out-of-class learning contracts, correspondence courses, and prior learning portfolios.

Fees:
Application fee: $25.00
Early transcript evaluation fee: $25
Seminar fee: $400
Tuition per semester hour: $85
Annual pariticipation fee: $75
Reinstatement fee: $100
Portfolio evaluation fee (per portfolio): $150

Accreditation: Southern Association of Colleges and Schools

Residency: Students are required to be on campus once for a two-and-one-half day Adult Learning Seminar.

Narration:
The New College was established by The University of Alabama in 1971 to provide students with an alternative approach to the undergraduate educational experience. The External Degree Program assists adult students whose educational needs cannot be met by residential programs. Applicants must come to the campus only once to attend a two-and-one-half-day seminar that introduces the curriculum, the advising system, and degree planning procedures. A minimum of 32 semester hours for a degree must be completed under the guidance of the University of Alabama New College External Degree Program. University of Alabama credit may include on-campus courses, correspondence

128

courses, and credit for prior learning. Adult students have many opportunities to acquire learning through professional, civic, and personal experiences, and to design courses through Out-of-Class Learning Contracts that meet individual academic needs. Academic planning is conducted by telephone and written correspondence.

The University of Alabama offers a Depth Study Program, which is a student's chosen academic area of concentration that can be built around current or future occupation, personal interests, or a combination of the two. Students enrolled in this program will not complete a traditional major but rather will identify a minimum of 32 semester hours from interdisciplinary fields of study. Academic planning is conducted by telephone and written correspondence.

UNIVERSITY OF COLORADO / COLORADO SPRINGS

Contact:
University of Colorado at Colorado Springs
Division of Continuing Education
P.O. Box 7150
Colorado Springs, Colorado 80933-7150

Telephone:
719-593-3364

Degrees Offered: no complete degree programs; a variety of classes offered that may be applied to degrees

Summary: Many standard courses are offered to off-campus students via live, interactive cable television; course offerings vary from semester to semester

Fees:
Same as for regular University of Colorado classes:
Admission fee: $40
Tuition (in-state, for Arts and Sciences):
Undergraduate   Graduate

1-3 credit hours: $387	1-3 credit hours: $465
4 credit hours: $516	4 credit hours: $620
5 credit hours: $645	5 credit hours: $775
6 credit hours: $774	6 credit hours: $930
7 credit hours: $903	7 credit hours: $1,085
8 credit hours: $1,032	8 credit hours: $1,240
9-18 credit hours: $1,061	9-18 hours: $1,395

Accreditation: North Central Association of Colleges and Schools

Residency: none; students must live within range of Colorado Springs Cablevision or CENCOM Cable

Narration:

Off-campus students may participate in live, interactive, credit-bearing classes over the CU-NET instructional television system (broadcast via Colorado Springs Cablevision and CENCOM Cable). Broadcast courses consist of regular classes with the addition of a broadcast and cablecast element. Off-campus students will have the same access to the instructor as do on-campus students through a standard telephone link, and will be able to ask any questions as they arise. Students follow the same syllabus and meet the same course requirements as in-class students.

CU-NET course offerings vary semester-to-semester. Each college is given the opportunity to schedule CU-NET courses, and student requests are taken into consideration when scheduling classes.

Among the Colorado Springs companies/military institutions currently participating in the CU-NET system are Hewlett Packard, Digital Equipment Corporation, Ampex, Loral Command and Control Systems, NCR, and Peterson Air Force Base.

UNIVERSITY OF DURHAM

Contact:
Durham University Business School
Mill Hill Lane
Durham City

DH1 3LB United Kingdom

Telephone:
091-374 -2219
International + 44 -91-374 -2219
FAX: 091-374 -3389
FAX: International + 44-91-374 -3389

Degrees Offered: Master's of Business Administration (M.B.A.)

Summary: M.B.A. may be earned while pursuing career; program provides complete flexibility in the event of job or location changes.

Fees: (Fees are approximate, depending on the current exchange rate)
Stage 1: $2,475   Fee covers registration, examinations, self-contained distance learning course material and personal tuition.
Stage 2: $2,775 Fee covers registration, examinations, tuition for the residential seminar, distance learning course material including essential text books, study notes, audio cassettes and personal tuition.
Stage 3: $2,775   Fee covers all items listed under Stage 2.
Stage 4: $1,650 Fee covers registration, project supervision and assessment.

Residency: limited; one intensive residential session

Narration:
Founded in 1832, Durham University is the third oldest university in England (after Cambridge and Oxford). The Open Distance Learning M.B.A. is highly commended by the British Institute of Management as being one of the top four degrees of this kind offered in the United Kingdom. Applicants must have at least three years of managerial work experience. The course is usually studied over a three or four year period.
An intellectually rigorous program, the M.B.A. is designed to improve the personal effectiveness of practicing managers. With open distance learning, the student undertakes a work-related project concentrating on a problem or opportunity in his/her own company, under the guidance of a project supervisor. The M.B.A.

131

program has four stages: 1) The Company/Individual Perspective, 2) The Industry Perspective, 3) and 4) The International Perspective.

UNIVERSITY OF IDAHO ENGINEERING OUTREACH

Contact:
University of Idaho
Engineering Outreach
Janssen Engineering Building
Moscow, Idaho 83844-1014

Telephone:
208-885-6373
Toll free: 800-824-2889
FAX: 208-885-6165

Degrees Offered: Master of Science (M.S.) in Agricultural Engineering, Civil Engineering, Computer Science, Computer Engineering, Electrical Engineering, Geological Engineering, Mechanical Engineering, or Psychology with an emphasis in Human Factors

Summary: Video-based graduate degree courses mainly in engineering; students work independently during the regular university semester

Fees:
Tuition (per credit)
          Undergraduate courses and nonmatriculated students: $259
          Admitted graduate students and all 500-level courses: $283

Accreditation: Northwest Association of Schools and Colleges; Accreditation Board for Engineering and Technology

Residency: none

Narration:

The Engineering Outreach Program facilitates off-campus delivery of Master's Degree programs in engineering and psychology. A thesis option and a nonthesis option are available for each degree. Courses in mathematics, statistics, and several other subjects are also offered.

All courses are regular college-level courses which have been professionally videotaped in a studio classroom setting at the University of Idaho. Most courses are current—they will be taped during the upcoming semester. Videotapes are shipped weekly throughout the 16-week semester along with related class hand-outs. Examinations are sent directly to an examination coordinator recommended by the student, who is responsible for supervising the examination process and returning it. Classes are not self paced—students are expected to maintain normal progress in the class by staying no more than two weeks behind the on-campus schedule. Students may contact their instructors through a toll-free telephone line, by fax, or through electronic mail. Access to internet is necessary in order to communicate through E-Mail.

UNIVERSITY OF ILLINOIS AT URBANA-CHAMPAIGN

Contact:
Guided and Individual Study
Office of Continuing Education and Public Service
University of Illinois at Urbana-Champaign
Suite 1406, 302 East John Street
Champaign, Illinois 61820

Telephone:
217-333-1321

Degrees Offered: No complete degree programs are offered through correspondence; however, students working toward a bachelor's degree from the University of Illinois or other schools may earn up to 60 semester hours by correspondence instruction; over 130 credit courses in 26 subjects are available.

Summary: Large number and variety of correspondence courses;

no complete degree programs

Fees:
Expense fee: $20
Study Guide fee: $18
Tuition: (per semester credit hour): $63

Accreditation: North Central Association of Schools and Colleges

Residency: none for correspondence courses

Narration:
Guided Individual Study provides instruction on an individual basis to people who cannot come to campus to study. Individuals learn at their own pace using instructional materials designed for independent study. Courses may make use of printed study guides, slides, textbooks, audio tapes and videotapes, broadcast radio and television, telephone, and computer. Student contact with the instructor is maintained by mail. A student may enroll at any time, study at home, and maintain an individual schedule. Upon enrollment, the student receives a study guide that includes a list of required textbooks and materials, study instructions, supplementary information, and specific learning assignments. Examinations must be taken under the supervision of an authorized proctor.

UNIVERSITY OF IOWA

Contact:
Guided Correspondence Study
The University of Iowa
116 International Center
Iowa City, Iowa 52242-1802

Telephone:
319-335-2575
Toll free: 800-272-6430
FAX: 319-335-2740

Degrees Offered: Bachelor of Liberal Studies (B.L.S.)

Summary: Undergraduate degree program with a broad range of study areas; available entirely through correspondence study

Fees:
Enrollment fee (per course): $15
Tuition (per semester hour): $68

Accreditation: North Central Association of Colleges and Schools

Residency: none

Narration:

The Bachelor of Liberal Studies program has five distribution areas from which the student selects three in place of a major. The areas are: Communication/Arts, Humanities, Natural Sciences/Math, Social Sciences, and Professional Fields (Business, Education, Physical Education, Medical Fields, Social Work, Counseling, Engineering, Leisure Studies, Museology, Speech Pathology, Dentistry, Pharmacy, Library Science, Nursing, or Urban Planning).

Through Guided Correspondence Study, students earn university credit at their own pace, taking up to nine months to complete a course. Enrollment can take place at any time during the year. The independent study format provides a great opportunity to develop a one-to-one relationship with the instructor. Bachelor of Liberal Studies students can apply an unlimited number of correspondence study hours to their degree requirement; for other undergraduate programs at the University of Iowa up to 30 hours of Guided Correspondence Study credit may be applied toward a degree. Credit may be awarded for prior knowledge by means of standardized examinations.

UNIVERSITY OF LONDON

Contact:
The External Programme
Room 264, Senate House

University of London
Malet Street
London WC1E 7HU
UK

Telephone:
071-636-8000 ext. 3150
FAX: 071-636-5894

Degrees Offered: Undergraduate: Bachelor of Laws (L.L.B.); Bachelor of Arts (B.A.) in English, German, Philosophy, Spanish & Latin American Studies, Jewish History, French, Italian, and Geography; Diploma in Economics; Bachelor of Science (B.Sc.) in Economics, Mathematical Studies, Computing and Information Systems, Nursing Studies, and Management; Bachelor of Divinity (B.D.); Bachelor of Music (B.Mus.); Advanced Diploma in Education.
Postgraduate: Master of Arts (M.A.) and Diploma (in Distance Education); Master of Arts (M.A.) in Geography; Master of Science (M.Sc.) and Diploma in Agricultural Development, Environmental Management, Organizational Behavior, Occupational Psychology, and Financial Economics; Master of Science in Financial Management and Diploma in Financial Policy; Master of Laws (L.L.M.); Master of Science in Dental Radiology; Master of Science in Community Dental Practice.
Research: Master of Philosophy (M.Phil) and Doctor of Philosophy (Ph.D.)

Summary: Degrees obtained by examination (some degrees also require written papers). No correspondence courses are offered; programs offer reading lists and study guides and some programs provide comprehensive study packages backed by tutorial support.

Fees: Undergraduate students pay a handling fee for their initial application, registration fees annually and examination fees as appropriate. Fees vary according to the degree and the location of the student. For example, the cost of a typical Bachelor's degree is $2250 for students within the European Community and $2550 for students outside of the European Community.

Residency: none

Narration:

The University of London, which is a federation of over fifty colleges and institutes, has two kinds of student—Internal and External. External students may undertake their studies anywhere in the world and may decide for themselves how they prepare for examinations. The External Programme has been operating since 1858, and today has more than 20,000 registered students in over a hundred countries, with 5,000 new registrations each year. The standard of the degree awarded to both Internal and External students is the same—the University is bound by its Statutes to ensure that all candidates attain the same academic standard.

External students work at their own pace and to their own schedule, and are free to choose the place and method of study best suited to their personal circumstances. Some students prepare for examinations totally by themselves. The External Programme itself provides registered students with introductory study materials, but these are not extensive except in the case of some Master's degrees. For some undergraduate courses we supply reading lists and past examination papers only; for others we provide more detailed subject guides or introductions. However, this is not a correspondence and tutorial system. External students are responsible for organizing their own studies, using the materials we provide as a starting point.

Examinations are held at a number of centers in the United Kingdom, the Republic of Ireland and most other countries. Overseas examinations are usually organized through the local Ministry of Education or the British Council. Examinations are held worldwide in late May/early June each year.

UNIVERSITY OF MARYLAND

Contact:
University of Maryland University College
Bachelor's Degree-at-a-Distance

University Boulevard at Adelphi Road
College Park, Maryland 20742-1660

Telephone:
Toll free: 800-283-6832

Degrees Offered: Bachelor of Arts (B.A.), Bachelor of Science
(B.S.), paralegal document

Summary: Non-resident undergraduate degree programs for
students residing in the United States

Fees:
Application fee: $25
Tuition, undergraduate (per semester hour):
    Residents of Maryland: $160
    Nonresidents of Maryland: $175

Accreditation: Middle States Association of Colleges and Schools

Residency: none

Narration:
    The Bachelor's Degree-at-a-Distance program permits
maximum flexibility in scheduling, since no class sessions are
required and course examinations may be taken in proctored
settings near the student's location. To participate in this program, a student must physically reside within the United States,
including Alaska and Hawaii.
    The University is a member of the National Universities
Degree Consortium, an association of 10 major universities whose
purpose is to provide a bachelor's degree-completion program
using national cable television and satellite technologies. The
degree conferred by the University of Maryland through the
consortium is the Bachelor of Arts or Bachelor of Science with
primary concentration in management. Students pursuing this
degree take their primary courses with the University of Maryland,
but may take other supporting courses to earn credit toward
graduation through any of the other nine participating consortium
universities. Credit earned from these universities represents
transfer credit to a University of Maryland degree.

Other degree areas of concentration are: Behavioral and Social Sciences, Computer Science, Computer Studies, Fire Science, Management, Management Studies, Paralegal Studies, and Technology and Management. Courses are also available in Communication, English, General Science, Humanities, Information Systems Management, and Mathematics.

UNIVERSITY OF MASSACHUSETTS—AMHERST

Contact:
Video Instructional Program
113 Marcus Hall
College of Engineering
University of Massachusetts
Amherst, Massachusetts 01003

Telephone:
413-545-0063
FAX: 413-545-1227
Internet e-mail address: vip@ecs.umass.edu

Degrees Offered: Master of Science (M.S.) in Electrical and Computer Engineering or Engineering Management; some courses for the Doctor of Philosophy (Ph.D.) in Electrical and Computer Engineering

Summary: Videotaped engineering courses plus assignments, notes, and exams delivered to corporate sites on a weekly basis

Fees:
Tuition (3-credit course): $1,050

Accreditation: New England Association of Colleges and Schools; Accreditation Board of Engineering and Technology

Residency: Videotaped classes offered at corporate sites throughout the world

139

Narration:

The Video Instructional Program brings engineering courses to engineering professionals at corporate sites throughout the world. Engineering courses are videotaped and broadcast as they are being taught to an on-campus class, and sent to corporate sites on a weekly basis along with assignments, notes and exams. Students may communicate directly with faculty during live broadcasts, reserved phone hours, or via electronic mail. Students may enroll in individual courses, complete a graduate degree program, or audit courses on a non-credit basis.

Courses are also delivered by satellite transmission in cooperation with the National Technological University. Courses can be viewed during actual class time, and a two-way audio bridge allows the student to phone in questions during the live broadcast.

===

UNIVERSITY OF MINNESOTA/SCHOOL OF PUBLIC HEALTH

Contact:
University of Minnesota
ISP
Division of Health Management and Policy
School of Public Health
D-305, Box 97 Mayo Building
420 Delaware Street S.E.
Minneapolis, Minnesota 55455-0381

Telephone:
612-624-1411

Degrees Offered: Credential of Management Studies; or Credential of Advanced Studies (graduate level credits) which, upon separate admission, may be applied toward a Master's degree option at the University of Minnesota.

Summary: Professional programs for adults already employed in the health care field: Ambulatory Care Administration; Hospital and Healthcare Administration; and Patient Care Administration

140

Fees:
Course fees (per year): $2,520

Accreditation: ISP is accredited via its master's options: the Master's in Public Health (M.P.A.) is accredited by the Council for Education on Public Health, the Master's in Health Administration (M.H.A.) by the Accrediting Commission on Education for Health Services Administration. ISP is also accredited as part of the School of Public Health and the University of Minnesota at large.

Residency: Limited

Narration:

ISP is designed for the adult learner employed as a health services administrator. Eligibility is based on the administrator's job responsibility and accountability. The courses are designed to develop the philosophical attitudes and skills of administrators while allowing for immediate application to issues of their organizations. Physicians and other clinically prepared people who spend 50% or more time in administrative positions are welcome.

Courses cover management within the health-care organization, administrative and professional relationships, and the external forces influencing the healthcare delivery system. The multi-method learning combines a two-week residential session with monthly student/preceptor meetings in the student's geographic area, written assignments and regional seminars.

Ambulatory Care Administration

Ambulatory Care is expected to improve the quality, cost control and effectiveness of health-care delivery. The program serves ambulatory care administrators who want to build knowledge and skills to meet this challenge while remaining in full time positions. Administrative skills useful in one's own organization are emphasized, building performance for those without formal education as well as those with graduate degrees.

Hospital and Healthcare Administration

This program was created to help administrators develop and maintain professional excellence while remaining in their administrative roles. The program enables practitioners without formal education, as well as those with graduate degrees, to build capabilities in areas related to actual performance.

Patient Care Administration
　　The program provides nurse executives an opportunity to strengthen leadership through knowledge and skills while remaining in full time positions. The curriculum spans a broad range of relevant executive topics including organizational behavior, problem solving, human resource development, and financial management.

UNIVERSITY OF MISSOURI—COLUMBIA

Contact:
University of Missouri
Center for Independent Study
136 Clark Hall
Columbia, Missouri 65211

Telephone: 314-882-2491
Exam Information: 314-882-2072
FAX: 314-882-6808

Degrees Offered: Bachelor of Science (B.S.) in General Agriculture; for other degrees a student may earn, with approval, at least 30 hours of credit by correspondence.

Summary: Bachelor of Science (B.S.) degree in General Agriculture may be earned through Nontraditional Study Program; wide range of correspondence courses for partial degree fulfillment offered through the Center for Independent Study.

Fees:
Tuition (per credit hour):
　　Undergraduate: $91.10
　　Graduate: $115.30
Tuition for out-of-state students is the same as for Missouri residents.

Accreditation: North Central Association of Colleges and Schools

142

Residency: None for classwork; exams must be taken under supervision at a University location.

Narration:

The Center for Independent Study was established in 1911. Today it is one of the largest independent study programs in the nation, with more than 18,000 new enrollments each year. Students come from every state in the nation, as well as more than a dozen foreign countries.

Correspondence courses are offered in a wide variety of fields, including liberal arts, animal sciences, physical sciences, computer science, criminology, education, engineering, health services management, and parks, recreation and tourism. The Nontraditional Study Program offers a bachelor's degree program in general agriculture through extended learning. This program offers credit for examinations in certain subjects as well as recognizing military and portfolio credits for prior learning.

Course exams must be taken under the direct supervision of a staff member at a University of Missouri County Extension Center. Exams may also be taken at the University of Missouri Extension office on the Rolla campus, at the Continuing Education offices on the Kansas City campus, and at the Center for Independent Study facilities located on the Columbia campus. Students who have serious difficulty in scheduling examinations at one of the above locations may request an exception allowing the examination to be supervised by a faculty member of an accredited university or college.

UNIVERSITY OF NORTH CAROLINA AT CHAPEL HILL

Contact:
Graduate Programs in Health Policy and Administration
Department of Health Policy and Administration
School of Public Health
University of North Carolina
Chapel Hill, North Carolina 27599-7400

Telephone:
919-966-7359

Degrees Offered: Master of Healthcare Administration (M.H.A.),
Master of Public Health (M.P.H.)

Summary: Non-resident professional master's degree programs
for working healthcare professionals

Fees:
Application fee: $45
Tuition
      North Carolina resident: $1,368
      Non-resident: $7,888
Fees: $457

Accreditation: Accrediting Commission on Education for Health
Services Administration

Residency: Limited

Narration:
      The Executive Master's Program in the Department of
Health Policy and Administration offers the opportunity for working healthcare professionals to obtain a master's degree while
maintaining their full-time employment. This program offers
classes one full day per week at several off-campus sites.
      The Master of Healthcare Administration is a professional
degree for students wishing to pursue management careers in
hospitals, health departments, health maintenance organizations, group practices, insurance firms, consulting organizations,
and other healthcare settings. It is designed to provide strong
preparation in the management disciplines, a comprehensive
understanding of the healthcare sector, and an opportunity to
pursue an area of concentration. Students complete this degree
within four years.
      The Master of Public Health is intended for those students
who hold a doctoral or professional degree. Students gain a
comprehensive understanding of public health philosophy, methods, and values, pursue an area of concentration, and are prepared for management and policy-related careers in the health

sector. Both degrees are designed to meet the needs of working professionals who hold administrative or managerial positions in health care organizations. Students complete this degree within three years.

UNIVERSITY OF NEBRASKA—LINCOLN

Contact:
University of Nebraska-Lincoln
Department of Distance Education
157 Nebraska Center for Continuing Education
Lincoln, Nebraska 68583

Telephone:
402-472-1924
FAX: 402-472-1901

Degrees Offered: none; the University is affiliated with two other degree-granting institutions to which credit may be transferred for degrees

Summary: Independent study courses, no degree programs; credit is recognized at affiliated institutions

Fees:
Tuition (per credit hour): $73.25
Handling fee (for each course enrollment: $17.50

Accreditation: North Central Association of Colleges and Schools

Residency: none

Narration:
Designed for students who cannot pursue post-secondary education in a traditional classroom setting, the Department of Independent Study has received 42 awards for course design excellence from the National University Continuing Education Association. Although the University does not offer an external

degree program, there is affiliation with two other external degree-granting institutions: Thomas Edison State College of Trenton, New Jersey, and the University of the State of New York Regents College in Albany, New York. Both institutions have preapproved University of Nebraska-Lincoln independent study courses for transfer and application to their degree programs.

Course offerings for non-credit include a real estate training program, building inspection, and refresher courses in math and English.

Credit courses include a wide variety of liberal arts offerings as well as agricultural topics, broadcasting, family and consumer science, health and human performance, industrial management systems engineering, business, and physical sciences.

UNIVERSITY OF NEVADA

Contact:
Division of Continuing Education
University of Nevada, Reno
Reno-Nevada 89557-0032

Telephone: 702-784-4652
Toll free: 800-233-8928

Degrees Offered: Bachelor of General Studies Degree; Baccalaureate degree programs in Clinical Laboratory Sciences, Health Care Administration and Health Physics; Master's degree programs in Physical Therapy and Nursing; undergraduate correspondence courses in liberal arts

Summary: Correspondence study courses in a wide variety of liberal arts fields as well as professional programs

Fees:
Tuition (per credit): $60

Accreditation: Northwest Association of Schools and Colleges

Residency: none

Narration:

The University of Nevada, Las Vegas and the University of Nevada, Reno offer an Independent Study by Correspondence program through the Division of Continuing Education. The program offers an individualized method of learning that uses a course syllabus, textbooks, video and audio cassettes, and additional reference and instructional material. No class attendance is necessary. Students have a year from the date of enrollment to complete each course. All courses have a final examination which must be taken in a proctored situation. The Bachelor of General Studies degree program includes courses in Humanities and Fine Arts, Natural Sciences, Social Sciences, Communication and English Composition.

The University of Nevada, Las Vegas's College of Health Sciences offers a Health Care Administration program that trains health care professionals. In the College of Hotel Administration, ten courses in Hotel Administration are offered through the independent study-correspondence course format.

UNIVERSITY OF NORTH DAKOTA

Contact:
University of North Dakota
Correspondence Study
Division of Continuing Education
P.O. Box 9021
Grand Forks, North Dakota 58202-9021

Telephone:
701-777-3044
Toll free: 800-342-8230
FAX: 700-777-4282

Noncredit correspondence study:
701-777-4204
Toll free: 800-342-8230

Degrees Offered: none; correspondence courses in Liberal Arts, Business and Vocational Education, Engineering, Industrial Technology, Computer Science, Economics, Fine Arts, Music, Occupational Therapy, Pharmacology and Toxicology. Noncredit courses in Nutrition and Food Service topics, Real Estate subjects

Summary: Credit and non-credit correspondence courses in a variety of fields

Fees:
Credit correspondence courses (per credit hour): $70
Noncredit courses vary from $40 to $260 (per course)

Accreditation: North Central Association of Colleges and Schools

Residency: none

Narration:

Courses for academic credit are offered through Credit Correspondence Study. Correspondence study assists persons who wish to pursue college courses in settings outside the traditional college classroom. The year-round college-level courses are similar in scope and content to those taught on campus. Correspondence study is a highly accessible and flexible learning experience; students can study at any time and any place. Without classroom interaction, a course can be very challenging.

Correspondence courses are offered in Accounting, Anthropology, Business and Vocational Education, Chemical Engineering, Computer Science, Economics, Engineering, English Language and Literature, Fine Arts, Geography, History, Home Economics, Humanities, Industrial Technology, Languages, Management, Mathematics, Music, Occupational Therapy, Pharmacology and Toxicology, Philosophy and Religious Studies, Political Science, Psychology, Sociology, and Visual Arts. Noncredit courses are available in a variety of Dietary Management, Nutrition, and Food Service topics, as well as Real Estate, Mortgage, and Property Management subjects.

UNIVERSITY OF OKLAHOMA

Contact:
The University of Oklahoma
College of Liberal Studies
1700 Asp Avenue
Norman, Oklahoma 73072-9985

Telephone:
405-325-1061
Toll free: 800-522-4389

Degrees Offered: Bachelor of Liberal Studies (B.L.S.), Master of Liberal Studies (M.L.S.)

Summary: Self-paced study at home with faculty guidance; brief, intensive seminars on campus once each year; interdisciplinary learning

Fees:
Admission fee: $65
Tuition (per credit hour):
Bachelor's degree

	Residents	Nonresidents
Lower Division (per credit hour)	$51.10	$ 159.10
Lower Division (per credit hour)	$54.34	$ 176.11

Master's degree

Introductory Seminar:	$281.40	$ 878.64
Directed Study:	$633.15	$1,976.94
Colloquium:	$422.10	$1,317.96
Advanced Study:	$633.15	$1,976.94
Advanced Seminar:	$281.40	$ 878.64

Accreditation: North Central Association of Colleges and Schools

Residency: Limited

Narration:
      The College of Liberal Studies provides coherent, interdisciplinary, liberal arts programs through innovative formats that

serve the needs of nontraditional students. Each student moves through the program at a self-determined pace. Knowledge attained from previous academic achievements, professional activities, and life experiences affect the amount of time spent in each study area. For independent study, a student works closely with a faculty advisor—a different one for each area of study—who outlines the expectations of the study program, provides tutorial guidance, and evaluates progress. The student communicates with the advisor by letter, telephone, e-mail, or personal appointments.

The College of Liberal Studies requires only three seminars on campus for a bachelor's degree: a five-day seminar to get started, and two ten-day seminars before completing degree requirements. Students may complete independent study assignments at home for the remainder of the requirements. There are three broad topic areas of study: humanities, natural sciences and social sciences. Detailed study guides are provided, and faculty advisors outline reading and writing assignments.

The Master of Liberal Studies emphasizes interdisciplinary learning, stressing the relationships of knowledge in the larger context of knowing and behaving. There is no set body of content for students to follow: the student becomes involved in the development of an individualized learning plan incorporating personal needs, interests, and goals. This degree program departs from conventional graduate program procedures by permitting great flexibility for the student to progress at a pace according to his or her personal circumstances. Advancement is made by completing self-directed independent study and on-campus intensive seminar steps rather than by attending conventional classes.

UNIVERSITY OF PHOENIX

Contact:
University of Phoenix
Center for Distance Education
4615 E. Elwood St.
Phoenix, Arizona 85040

Telephone:
602- 921-8014
Toll free: 800-366-9699

Degrees Offered:
Associate of Arts (A.A.) in Business, Bachelor of Science (B.S.) in Business Administration or Nursing; Bachelor of Arts (B.A.) in Management; Master of Business Administration (M.B.A.); Master of Arts (M.A.) in Organizational Management; Master of Nursing (M.N.); Master of Arts (M.A.) in Education

Summary: Undergraduate and graduate degree programs in a wide variety of fields. Students have ten weeks to finish each class and can communicate with faculty by mail, telephone, and teleconferencing.

Fees:
Application fee: $50
Undergraduate:
      curriculum tuition per credit:
      directed study: $210
      teleconferencing: $225
Graduate:
      curriculum tuition per credit:
      directed study: $240
      teleconferencing: $275
Graduation audit fee: $50
Other fees may apply

Accreditation: North Central Association of Colleges and Schools; National League for Nursing

Residency: none

Narration:
     The University of Phoenix offers undergraduate and graduate degree programs that are designed for working professionals. The Directed Study program offers access to higher education for students who are faced with schedule or location constraints. The courses cover the same material and use the same textbooks as regular classroom courses. Students are given a course syllabus

at the time of enrollment, and have 10 weeks to complete each course. Students work with a faculty member by telephone, voice mail, fax and mail systems. In geographic areas not served by a Phoenix University campus, students may participate in degree programs through classroom-based live interactive teleconferencing, which permits students and faculty to join in active discussions while viewing slides and other visual materials. Each class meets once a week and has an on-site facilitator.

Another option provided by the University of Phoenix is the Online computer-based educational delivery system, a computer conferencing system that enables students and faculty to engage in individual and group conversations at any time or from any place. Rather than gathering in a classroom, students and instructors interact electronically through the student's own personal computer. Interaction is asynchronous, enabling the student to participate at any time. Research has shown that in the online learning environment, adult learners participate much more than in a regular classroom and are much more actively involved in their own educations.

The University of Phoenix emphasizes an integration of theory and practice, with curriculum designed in cooperation with the business, industry, or profession to which the particular degree program relates.

The University of Phoenix recognizes college-level learning acquired through experience, and Prior Learning Credit of up to 30 undergraduate semester hours may be awarded as a result of professional training or experience.

UNIVERSITY OF SANTA BARBARA

Contact:
University of Santa Barbara
Administrative Offices
4050 Calle Real
Santa Barbara, California 93110

Telephone: 805-569-1024
FAX: 805-967-6289

Degrees Offered: Master of Arts (M.A.) in Education, Doctor of Education (Ed.D.), Doctor of Philosophy (Ph.D.) in Education; Master of Science (M.S.) in Business Administration, Finance, International Business, Management, Marketing; Master of Business Administration (M.B.A.), Doctor of Philosophy (Ph.D.) in Business Administration.

Summary: Limited residency graduate programs in the fields of education and business

Fees:
Tuition (per year): $4,200 (some variation according to program)

Accreditation: undergoing accreditation process with Pacific Association of Colleges and Schools

Residency: Limited; resident seminars in research development held annually during July

Narration:

The University of Santa Barbara was founded to meet the academic aspirations and professional needs of qualified men and women who elect to pursue an advanced degree while, at the same time, meeting their current professional commitments. The University is dedicated to education at the graduate level in the form of guided, independent study and research based on the tutorial method. Resident seminars in research development and pertinent issues related to the student's academic focus are conducted during the month of July in Santa Barbara.

All courses of study contain an international studies component and an ethics emphasis. Instructional modalities include communication by fax and teleconferencing.

Programs in Education may include a concentration in: Adult Education, Child Development and Learning, Curriculum and Supervision, Educational Counseling, Educational Foundations, Educational Psychology, Gifted Child Education, International Studies for Educators, Reading and Reading Disability, School Administration, Special Education, Teaching Methods (in a content area), or Health-Care Education.

Programs in Business may include a concentration in Administration, Finance, Management, Marketing, or International Business.

UNIVERSITY OF WISCONSIN—EXTENSION

Contact:
University of Wisconsin-Extension
Independent Study
209 Extension Building
432 North Lake Street
Madison, Wisconsin 53706-1498

Telephone:
Toll free: 800-442-6460
FAX: 608-262-4096

Degrees Offered: No degree programs through Extension; external degree programs offered through University of Wisconsin campuses

Summary: Wide range of correspondence courses for undergraduate university credit, continuing education, high school credit, professional and vocational study

Fees:
Independent Study registration fee: $30
Tuition:
>University credit courses (per credit): $53
>Vocational credit courses (per credit): $43.65

Accreditation: North Central Association of Schools and Colleges

Residency: none

Narration:
>The Independent Study program offers nearly 600 correspondence courses for university, high school, continuing education, and vocational-technical credit. A student can start a course at any time, study at his/her own pace, and get one-on-one help from the instructor through the mail. The course guide directs

students through coursework, gives help, and assigns written work for each unit of study. A course will also use textbooks and, possibly, audiocassettes, records, kits of materials, videocassettes, slides, films, computer disks, or radio and television broadcasts.

UNIVERSITY OF WISCONSIN—GREEN BAY

Contact:
Extended Degree, ES109
University of Wisconsin-Green Bay
Green Bay, Wisconsin 54301-7001

Telephone:
414-465-2423

Degrees Offered: Bachelor's degree in General Studies with Individualized Area of Emphasis

Summary: Individualized degree program with a focus uniquely designed for each student; supervised independent learning; assessment of prior learning

Accreditation: North Central Association of Colleges and Schools

Residency: Limited

Narration:
This extended degree program is highly individualized and is designed for adults who are interested in career changes, personal enrichment, or job promotions. Students can design professionally oriented academic programs within a liberal arts framework. All of the courses required for the degree are self-paced and take several forms: learning guides; individualized learning contracts; weekend seminars; and Summer Week. In all learning activities, students maintain contact with professors through periodic meetings, written correspondence, or phone calls. Each student designs an Area of Emphasis that focuses on a topic of special interest.

A student who has experience equivalent to college level learning may be able to use it for degree credit. Learning based on experience can include: employment, on-the-job training, armed services training, and volunteer activities. An additional way to earn college credit is through testing out of a course.

UNIVERSITY OF WISCONSIN—MADISON

Contact:
Department of Engineering Professional Development
The College of Engineering
University of Wisconsin-Madison
432 North Lake Street
Madison, Wisconsin 53706-1498

Telephone:
608-262-2061
608-262-0133
Toll free: 800-462-0876
FAX: 608-263-3160

Degrees Offered: Professional Development (P.D.) Degree in Engineering

Summary: Professional degree alternative to a Master's of Science degree; allows practicing engineers to earn degree while maintaining careers

Fees:
Application fee: $20
Course fees vary according to type; a typical program costs between $2500-$4500.
Independent Study Project: $600

Accreditation: North Central Association of Colleges and Schools

Residency: none

Narration:

The Professional Development Degree in Engineering is an advanced degree, an alternative to the M.S. degree that allows practicing engineers to earn a post-baccalaureate degree without leaving their current position to return to campus. A degree candidate may reside anywhere in the world. All degree requirements can be completed via distance learning formats such as correspondence courses, video tape courses, satellite and other telecommunication methods, and courses on campus in the candidate's geographical area. A required independent study project offers candidates an opportunity to integrate new knowledge acquired from coursework into a practical learning experience, guided and evaluated by a faculty advisor.

Students may design their own program of study; with this option all degree requirements may be completed through correspondence and independent study courses. Alternatively, a student may complete one of the six focus areas: disaster management, electrical engineering, energy management, manufacturing technology, public works, or value engineering. Some of the focus programs require candidates to complete a few two- to five-day continuing education courses on the Madison campus.

UNIVERSITY OF WISCONSIN—RIVER FALLS

Contact:
Extended Degree Program
College of Agriculture
University of Wisconsin-River Falls
River Falls, Wisconsin 54022

Telephone:
715-425-3239
Toll free: 800-228-5421
FAX: 715-425-3785

Degrees Offered: Bachelor of Science (B.S.) in agriculture or agricultural business

Summary: Undergraduate degree programs in agriculture primarily through home study; credit awarded for experiential learning

Fees:
Annual Service Agreement fee: $50
Prior learning assessment: 1-8 credits, $50; 9 or more credits, $100
Tuition (per credit)
      Wisconsin residents: $74.75
      Minnesota residents with reciprocity: $89
      Non-residents: $260

Accreditation: North Central Association of Colleges and Schools

Residency: Limited; periodic campus visits for certain courses

Narration:
Extended Degree Program courses are self-paced and are designed to be completed primarily at home with periodic campus visits depending on the courses selected. Students, in consultation with an advisor, select courses from the program to develop an individualized program within degree requirements. The courses are flexible yet academically demanding.

The student has opportunities to enroll throughout each term, not just at the beginning of a semester. An extended degree student may contract for as many as 18 semester credits each enrollment.

An important feature of the program is that students may receive university credit through assessment of their experiential learning. Credit is awarded for experiential learning that equates to college level learning in agriculturally-related areas. Possibilities for academic credit range from learning gained through union- or company-sponsored courses, job training, and studies completed during military service to learning gained on a volunteer project, in running a business, or on-the-job work experience. Credit may be granted for special military training programs.

Examinations for the program courses can be administered in the student's local area by an approved proctor, who returns the exams to the Program Office for grading. The Extended Degree Program provides some of the textbooks and course materials on a loan basis.

THE UNION INSTITUTE

Contact:
The Union Institute
440 East McMillan Street
Cincinnati, Ohio 45206-1947

Telephone:
513-861-6400
Toll free: 800-486-3116
FAX: 513-861-0779

Degrees Offered: Bachelor of Arts (B.A.), Bachelor of Science (B.S.), Doctor of Philosophy (Ph.D.)

Summary: Individualized programs of study that offer flexibility in meeting academic requirements; no prescribed courses; tutorial guided independent study

Fees:
Admissions fee: $50
Tuition (per semester credit hour):
         Sponsored learning: $205
Assessment fee for prior learning (per course): $150

Accreditation: North Central Association of Colleges and Schools

Residency: Limited; minimal number of residential seminar sessions throughout the year

Narration:
        The Union Institute was founded by ten college presidents as a vehicle for educational research and experimentation. It has developed a unique format for individualized programs of study that offer flexibility in meeting educational requirements by recognizing various methods of acquiring learning.
        The Center for Distant Learning was created to respond to the academic needs of learners who do not reside within close proximity to the Institute. Students participate fully in the development of an individualized program of study. Through tutorial guided study options and a minimum number of residen-

159

tial seminar meetings throughout the year, students may work independently with the help of the Institute's network of learning resources (library resources), and through computer conferencing and messaging.

Prior experiential learning may be evaluated for college credit. The student recalls and reviews past experience, organizes it by academic area, and presents it in a form that allows its evaluation for course equivalency at a university level. An Individual Learning Agreement concerns independent study with the guidance of a faculty sponsor. It is an agreement that outlines specific academic goals and objectives. This individualized plan may include the use of university courses, libraries, museums, private resources, professional associations, communication media, and any other services or materials needed and available. Carefully planned travel, conferences, workshops, lectures, experiences within professional work settings, and constructive social action may also become a part of the learner's strategy for academic and personal development.

The bachelor's degree program includes four areas of liberal learning: Humanities and Arts; Social Sciences; Language and Communications; and Natural Sciences and Mathematics. The graduate program is built around the concept of interdisciplinary studies. By working in more than one field, learners have the opportunity to locate their ideas in a variety of frames of reference. Students are encouraged to be keenly and continuously aware of the impact of the learning process on their lives. There are no prescribed courses, but each student's program is developed in consultation with faculty advisors to lead to proficiency in the student's fields of study.

UPPER IOWA UNIVERSITY

Contact:
Upper Iowa University
Division of Graduate and Continuing Studies
Alexander-Dickman Hall
P.O. Box 1861
Fayette, Iowa 52142

Telephone:
319-425-5252
Toll free: 800-553-4150
FAX: 319-425-5353

Degrees Offered: Associate of Arts (A.A.) in General Business; Bachelor of Science (B.S.) in Accounting, Management, Marketing, Public Administration, Human Services, and Social Science.

Summary: Undergraduate degrees through guided independent study

Fees:
Evaluation fee: $35
Tuition:
 Independent study (per semester hour): $120
Credit for experiential learning (per semester hour): $50

Accreditation: North Central Association of Colleges and Schools

Narration:

  The University recognizes learning acquired outside of the traditional college setting. A committee of faculty reviews supporting documents and awards credit for learning acquired as a result of accomplishments on the job, through volunteer work, training, workshops and seminars based upon time in service, job descriptions, supervisors' evaluations, relationship to the curriculum, and credit recommendations from the American Council on Education. Job-related experiential learning credit is evaluated based on two types of experience: training and work.

  Independent Study involves extensive reading and written answers to questions. Each assignment will be evaluated by the course instructor and returned with comments regarding individual assignments. A student may also submit comments and questions, creating a dialogue that parallels classroom instruction. Examinations must be supervised by a qualified person. Students may enroll at any time; a period of six months is allowed for completion of an independent study course.

VERMONT COLLEGE OF NORWICH UNIVERSITY

Contact:
Norwich University
Admissions Office
Vermont College
Montpelier, Vermont 05602

Telephone:
802-828-8500
Toll free: 800-336-6794
FAX: 802-828-8855

Degrees Offered: Bachelor of Arts (B.A.) in Liberal Studies; Master of Arts (M.A.)

Summary: Four-year self-designed undergraduate degree program with limited residency; flexible individually-designed master's degree program with no on-campus residency or required courses.

Fees:
Application fee: $35
Tuition per semester (undergraduate): $3,413

Accreditation: New England Association of Schools and Colleges

Residency: Undergraduate: one weekend a month or one 9-day residency each semester; graduate; no residency requirement but seminars held regionally

Narration:
The Adult Degree Program is a four-year college program of self-designed, guided inependent study. Students in the program carry fifteen credits per semester. There is a Weekend Option, with six weekend residencies during each semester, or a Nine Day Cycle Option, with a nine-day required residency on campus once every six months. Each semester students completes one inependent study project. Areas of study include: History, Business and Management, Economics, Literature and Writing, Education, Psychology, Art, Photography, Political Science, Anthropology, Religion, Natural Sciences, Women's Studies, Government, and Soci-

ology.

The Graduate Program consists of individually-designed degree work with no required courses. The program has no grades, exams or competitive hierarchy. Students define their own goals and then plan a program of study, exploring the literature of the chosen field while following a pragmatic approach of applying theory in real-life situations. Program seminars and colloquia are held regionally, with no on-campus residency requirement. Students are invited to propose studies in any aspect of the humanities, social sciences, the arts, and organizational development. Pamphlets are available to assist the student in conceptualizing a field of study in the following areas: Environmental Studies, Historical Studies, Interdisciplinary Studies, Studies in Literature and Writing, Master of Arts for Educators/Teacher Licensure, Master of Arts in Philosophy/Religious Studies, Organizational Development and Leadership Studies, Professional Counseling and Counseling Psychology, and Women's Studies/Multicultural Studies. The program has quarterly enrollment dates.

WALDEN UNIVERSITY

Contact:
Walden University
Processing Center
801 Anchor Rode Drive
Naples, Florida 33940

Telephone:
813-261-7277
Toll free: 800-444-6795

Degrees Offered: Doctor of Philosophy (Ph.D.) in Administration/Management, Health Services, and Human Services; Doctor of Education (Ed.D.)

Summary: Distance-learning doctoral programs; network of students and faculty with no fixed campus site

Fees:

Application fee: $50
Admission/Orientation Workshop Fee: $250
Course Material Fees: $250
Regional Session Fee (annual): $425
Summer Session Conference Fee (three week session): $730

Accreditation: North Central Association of Colleges and Schools

Residency: Limited; two weekends of intensive study (or one five-day session) each year, and one three-week summer session

Narration:
Walden offers mid-career professionals doctoral programs in Administration/ Management, Education, Health Services and Human Services. The program is specifically designed to allow students, in consultation with their faculty advisors, to tailor a program of study that integrates personal aspirations with the goals of the doctoral program. Upon completion of this plan, students begin the academic portion of the program, comprised of studying and demonstrating through research papers doctoral-level competence in several Knowledge Area Modules: Principles of Societal Development and the Future; Human Development; Organizational and Social Systems; and Research Design, Methodology and Theory.

In this university without walls, students do not convene on a regular basis in any one place; instead they engage in self-directed research in consultation with their faculty advisor. Walden students are required to attend two weekend Regional Intensive Sessions which are comprised of a series of workshops, lectures and one-on-one meetings between faculty and students. Students are also required to attend one three-week summer session held on the Bloomington campus of the University of Indiana.

Many doctoral candidates are in regular contact with other students and faculty by a state-of-the art electronic network.

WARWICK BUSINESS SCHOOL

Contact:

The University of Warwick
Coventry CV4 7AL
United Kingdom

Telephone:
Coventry 0203-524306
Telex: 317472 UNIREG
FAX: Coventry 0203-523719 or 524411

Degrees Offered: Master's of Business Administration (M.B.A.)

Summary: Distance learning graduate M.B.A. program

Fees:
Enrollment fee:
      Part A: $2880
      Part B: $2880
      Part C: $2880
      Part D: $1312

Accreditation: Association of M.B.A.s (professional association in the UK representing M.B.A. graduates from recognized business schools worldwide)

Residency: Limited; annual 8-day seminar

Narration:
      Designed for those who cannot study in residence, the Distance Learning route provides a flexible and portable mode of study. Study materials devised in-house exclusively for the program, combined with tutor support, local study groups and an annual residential seminar in September, enable participants to study according to their own schedules. Participants are spread across more than 70 countries worldwide, and up to 60% are sponsored by their employers.

      Many courses have open-book examinations designed to test the student's ability to apply the techniques and knowledge acquired in the course. Many subjects therefore include case study analysis, and expect students to draw on examples from their own workplace experience.

WASHINGTON SCHOOL OF LAW

Contact:
Washington School of Law
2268 East Newcastle Drive
Sandy, Utah 84093

Telephone:
801-943-2440

Degrees Offered: Master of Science in Taxation (M.S.Tax)

Summary: Graduate tax program offered entirely through external study and video tapes

Fees:
Tuition: $56 per scheduled lecture ($14 per classroom hour); total for full program: $5,000
Full program tuition payment plan discounts:
    $4,000 (paid in installments)
    $3,000 (paid in advance)
Mailing charge for videos (one-time fee):
    U.S.: $200
    Europe and Asia: $500

Accreditation: National Association of Private Nontraditional Schools and Colleges

Residency: none

Narration:
    The Master's Degree in Taxation is an advanced academic and professional degree; it is an interdisciplinary program for accountants and lawyers. It is an integrated program of texts and techniques offering advanced knowledge, expertise, and fulfillment of state continuing education requirements.
    The program is available to students entirely through external study and video tapes. Classes are recorded by tax lawyers in the live environment of an active in-residence classroom.

WASHINGTON STATE UNIVERSITY

Contact:
Washington State University
Extended Academic Programs
204 Van Doren Hall
Washington State University
Pullman, Washington 99164-5220

Telephone:
509-335-3557
Toll free: 800-222-4978
FAX: 509-335-0945

Degrees Offered: Bachelor of Arts (B.A.) in Social Sciences

Summary: Undergraduate degree program by videotape; some courses broadcast over Mind Extension University; print-based correspondence courses

Fees:
Tuition
> Correspondence courses (per credit hour): $90
> Extended Degree courses (per credit hour): $145

Video rental (per course): $44 or $80, depending on the number of tapes

Accreditation: Northwest Association of Schools and Colleges

Residency: None for correspondence courses; Extended Degree courses are available only to residents of Washington state; students residing outside of Washington must register through Mind Extension University, a national educational cable channel

Narration:
      The Correspondence and Extended Degree courses are distance learning options that provide the opportunity to pursue academic goals outside a traditional classroom setting. These distance learning courses offer flexible, convenient educational

alternatives to students able or needing to work independently.

Extended Degree courses are available regionally and follow a regular semester schedule. Students must start each course at the beginning of a semester and must complete the course within the 15-week semester. Students have regular assignments due at various intervals and generally have midterm and final examinations. Students must arrange for a proctor to monitor examinations. Students are expected to maintain regular contact with their instructors via voice mail, a toll-free telephone line, and written correspondence. A number of courses are broadcast over Mind Extension University, a cable television network. A limited number of course tapes may be rented from the University. Extended Degree courses include a variety of criminal justice topics, technical writing, business, and liberal arts subjects.

Students may enroll in correspondence courses at any time; all courses should be completed within one year of the date of enrollment. Correspondence courses are print-based. Subjects available through correspondence include business, liberal arts, criminal justice, family studies, food science, education, mathematics, and the sciences.

UNIVERSITY OF WATERLOO

Contact:
Correspondence Program
University of Waterloo
Waterloo, Ontario
Canada N2L 3G1

Telephone:
519-888-4050
FAX: 519-746-6393
Telex: 069-55259

Degrees Offered: Bachelor of Arts (B.A.), Non-Major or in Classical Studies, Economics, English, Geography, History, Philosophy,

Psychology, Religious Studies, Social Development Studies, or Sociology; a four-year General B.A. in Classical Studies and Social Development Studies; an Honors B.A. in Classical Studies or English; Bachelor of Environmental Studies (B.E.S.) in Geography; Bachelor of Science (B.Sc.); Non-Major or Honors Science Program. Most courses for the BMath General Degree offered through correspondence. Other courses in Engineering and Applied Health Sciences are offered.

Summary: Bachelor's degree programs through correspondence; 300 correspondence courses available

Fees:
Tuition (per half-credit course): $228
Foreign students are charged approximately four to five times the amount of tuition that is charged to Canadian citizens

Residency: None; exams must be taken under the supervision of a proctor

Narration:
Correspondence study is a form of independent learning through which the student studies with limited assistance from instructors. There are three terms of study available throughout the year, with examinations scheduled at the end of each term. Students taking exams at distant locations under the supervision of a proctor must complete them during the scheduled exam weekend. Most correspondence courses consist of textbooks, printed notes and audio tapes; an increasing number also use video components. Some courses have microscope slides, photographic prints, or 35 mm slides. A newsletter for correspondence students is published four times a year. Correspondence students may obtain a list of current students grouped by geographical region.

In addition to the degree programs, Waterloo offers diploma and certificate programs in Land Management for Land Surveyors, and Occupational Health Nursing. Short courses are available in Kinesiology, Urban and Regional Planning, and Certified Employee Benefits.

WEBER STATE UNIVERSITY

Contact:
Weber State University
Continuing Education and Community Service
Distance Learning
Ogden, Utah 84408-4005

Telephone:
801-626-6785
Toll free: 848-7770, Ext. 6785

Degrees Offered: Associate of Applied Science Respiratory Therapy; Associate of Science Respiratory Therapist, Bachelor of Science (B.S.) in Health Services Administration, Health Services Training and Promotion, Advanced Radiological Sciences, Advanced Dental Hygiene, or Respiratory Therapy. Certificate program in merchandising.

Summary: Correspondence courses leading to undergraduate degrees and certification in health-related fields.

Fees:
Application fee: $20
Tuition (per credit hour): $40

Accreditation: Northwest Association of Schools and Colleges; Radiological Sciences Programs are accredited by the American Medical Association

Residency: None; exams must be supervised by a proctor

Narration:
Weber State offers an accessible educational program that offers degrees and prepares health workers to become eligible for certification through self-directed independent study courses. In addition to Health Services Administration, specialized courses of study include Nuclear Medicine Technology, Respiratory Therapy, Dental Hygiene, Magnetic Resonance Imaging/Computed Tomography, and Diagnostic Medical Sonography.

Anyone may enroll in an independent study course, at any time of the year. It is recommended that students take only one correspondence course at a time. Students have six months to one year from the date of enrollment to complete an independent study course, depending on the field of study. If a student desires credit for a course, university admission requirements must be fulfilled prior to completing the first course. The courses are self-instructional and rely on textbooks, study guides, modules, video and audio tapes, and other learning aids prepared by the instructor to guide learning. Examinations must be taken under the supervision of a qualified proctor.

Correspondence courses are also offered in liberal arts subjects, business, criminal justice, computer topics, music, physical education, and sales and services technology.

WESTERN ILLINOIS UNIVERSITY

Contact:
Board of Governors Bachelor of Arts Degree Program
Non-Traditional Programs
5 Horrabin Hall
Western Illinois University
Macomb, Illinois 61455-1395

Telephone:
309-298-1929
FAX: 309-298-2226

Degrees Offered: Bachelor of Arts (B.A.)

Summary: Undergraduate degree program offered through independent study, prior learning assessment, and credit by examination; no major required

Fees:
Portfolio assessment: $30

Accreditation: North Central Association of Colleges and Schools

Narration:

The Board of Governors Bachelor of Arts Degree Program is a nontraditional approach to undergraduate education. It provides the student with an opportunity to earn an undergraduate degree in a manner compatible with his/her educational needs and lifestyle. By combining individually selected courses, a prior learning portfolio, and proficiency exams, a personalized program of study is created. This program does not require a major. The student is encouraged to take course work that meets individual educational needs. There is no time limit for completion of the degree program, but steady progress is expected of the student.

A portfolio documents prior learning that demonstrates knowledge of the subject matter taught in a university course. For example, if the student believes that a prior job in "accounts receivable" has taught many of the essentials of an introductory business course, college credit may be awarded if the student is able to demonstrate this knowledge in a portfolio. College credit may also be awarded for satisfactory scores on standardized examinations, as well as for certain military courses and training programs.

Independent Study Program courses are available through the mail. Each semester the Independent Study Program offers approximately 30 upper-division courses (including telecourses) in the humanities, social sciences, and natural sciences/mathematics.

Index

A

Acadia University.................... 18
Accounting72, 110, 116, 148, 161
Accreditation 4
Adam Smith University........... 19
Administration ..39, 45, 153, 163
    Ambulatory Care 140
    Health 81, 115, 125, 140, 144, 146, 170
    Hospital........................... 140
    Hotel 147
    of Justice......................... 105
    Office............................... 112
    Patient Care..................... 140
    Public 96, 161
    School 153
Adult Education.............. 85, 153
Adult Education Guided Independent Study (AEGIS) 47
Advertising Design 122
Aeronautical Science 54
Aesthetics 64
Ag Law 76
Agriculture 142, 157
    Business 157
    Development..................... 136
    Economics 75
    Engineering 43, 132
    Social Sciences 75
Agroecology 96
Allied Health 36
Ambulatory Care Administration. 140
America Online 53
American College 21
American College Testing Proficiency Exam Program 14
American College Testing Program 12
American Council on Education .. 1, 9, 14
American Psychological Association 4
American Studies 51
American University in London 22
Animal Ecology 75
Animal Sciences & Industry ... 76, 85, 143
Anthropology........... 64, 148, 162
Antioch University 24
Applied Arts 64
Applied Science & Technology 41, 123
Applied Studies 26
Art................................... 96, 162
Arts & Science 45
Associate Degrees 3
Astronomy 64
Athabasca University 25
Atlantic Union College 27

B

Bachelor's Degrees 3
Bastyr College 28
Behavioral Science 77, 87, 139
Bemidji State University 29
Berean College........................ 30
Bible 109
    & Missions 109
    & Practical Ministry 109
    & Theology 31
Biblical Foundations 79
Biology 64
    by Video 19
Botany 64
    Ethno 96
Brigham Young University 32
Building Inspection 146
Business ..19, 41, 50, 55, 64, 79, 82, 99, 114, 135, 148, 161, 168, 171
Business Administration ..18, 23,

37, 42, 43, 48, 64, 67, 74, 85, 86, 88, 93, 95, 101, 105, 110, 112, 115, 116, 119, 122, 123, 127, 131, 151, 153, 165

Aviation 54
Information Resources 74
Business, Agricultural 157
International 90, 153
Business Management 51, 72, 110, 162
Technology 91
Business Studies 23

C

Cable Courses 7
Caldwell College 34
California Coast University 37
California College for Health Sciences 35
California State University 33
Canadian Schools 18, 25, 85, 98, 168
Center for Degree Studies 71
Central Michigan University 38
Certified Employee Benefits ... 169
Charter Oak State College 40
Chartered Financial Consultant 21, 22
Chartered Life Underwriter 21, 22
Chemical Engineering 43, 148
Child Care 127
Child Development & Learning 153
Chinese Medicine 29
Chiropractic 19
Christian Counseling 31, 93
Christian Education 31, 109
Church
Assemblies of God 30, 109, 113
Catholic 83, 114, 116
Ministries 31, 79, 93, 114
Schools 18, 32, 48, 51, 79, 81, 93, 101
Seventh Day Adventist 27, 112
City University 41

Civil Engineering 43, 72, 132
Classical Studies 168
Clinical Laboratory Science ... 146
Clinical Sexology 70
Cohort Format 39
College Proficiency Programs ... 12
College-Level Examination Program 12, 14
Colorado State University 43
Colorado SURGE (State Univ Resources in Graduate Ed 44
Columbia Pacific University 45
Columbia Union Colleg 48
Columbia University/Teacher's College 46
Commerce 25, 42
Communication, Technical ... 103
Communications 50, 96, 102, 112, 135, 139, 147, 160
Community Dental Practice .. 136
Community Developement 39
Community Health Administra ... tion 36
Community Mental Health & Criminal Justice 87
Computer Engineering .. 132, 139
Computer Integrated Manufactur ing Systems Certificate 58
Computer Science 18, 19, 23, 41, 43. 64, 72, 74, 92, 103, 132, 139, 143, 148
Computer Software 99
Computer Studies 139, 171
Computer Technologies 74
Computing & Information Systems 136
Conflict Resolution 24
Construction Management Program 43
Cook's Institute of Electronic Engineering 50
Correspondence Courses 6
Council for Adult & Experiential Learning 9
Counseling 64, 135

Educational 153
Licensure Program 101
Professional 79, 163
Psychology 163
Creative Studies 66
Creative Writing 105
Credentials Evaluation Service 15
Criminal Justice 30, 87, 122, 168, 171
Criminology 143
Crop Conditioning & Handling 75
Curriculum & Supervision 153

D

Defense Activity for Non-Traditional Educational Support 14
Dental Hygiene 170
Dental Radiology 136
Dentistry 135
Diagnoltic Medical Sonography 170
Diet & Behavior 29
Dietary Management 148
Dietetic Food Systems Management 95
Disaster Management 157
Distance Learn 100
Docotorate Degrees 4

E

Early Reading Education Certificate 85
Earned College Credit for What You Know 9
Earth & Mineral Sciences 95
Eckerd College 51
Ecology Agro 96
Ecology Animal 75
Economics 86, 136, 148, 162, 168
Agricultural 75
Financial 136
Home 148
Education . 23, 27, 37, 39, 42, 43, 47, 50, 64, 77, 85, 88, 95, 102,
112, 116, 135, 136, 143, 151, 153, 162, 163, 168
Adult 153
Christian 109
Early Childhood 119
Elementary Christian School 94
Environmental 96
Gifted Child 153
Health Care 153
Physical 135, 171
Religious 81
Special 153
Teacher 96
Vocational 148
Educational Counseling 153
Educational Credential Evaluators, Inc. 15
Educational Foundations 153
Educational Psychology 153
Educational Technology Leadership Program 57, 58
Educational Testing Service 12
Electrical Engineering 43, 58, 72, 132, 139, 157
Electronic Campus 53
Electronic University Network . 53
Electronics Technologies ... 72, 99
Elementary Christian School Education 94
Embry-Riddle Aeronautical University 54
Empire State College 55
Energy Managment 157
Engineering .. 23, 37, 88, 95, 135, 143, 148, 157, 169
Agricultural 43, 132
Chemical 43, 148
Civil 43, 72, 132
Computer 132, 139
Electrical 43, 58, 72, 132, 139, 157
Environmental 43, 58
Geological 132
Industrial 43, 58, 72
Management Program . 43, 139

Manufacturing Systems 103
Mechanical 43, 72, 103, 132
Nuclear 58
Systems 43
Technology 61
Value 157
English . 23, 50, 64, 98, 112, 116, 119, 127, 136, 139, 146, 148, 168
Composition 147
Environmental Education 96
Environmental Engineering 43, 58
Environmental Management . 136
Environmental Sciences 64
Environmental Studies ... 96, 163, 169
Equine Studies 116
Erotology 70
Ethnobotany 96

F

Family 32
Family Studies 168
Finance 153
Financial Economics 136
Financial Management 136
Financial Policy 136
Financial Services 21
Fine Arts 34, 50, 64, 147, 148
Finite Mathematics 86
Fire Science Technology .. 41, 139
Fire Service Administration 55
Food Science 168, 148
Foreign Schools 22, 64, 130, 135, 164
Forensic Sexology 70
French 136

G

GED 85
General Agriculture 142
General Science 139
General Studies ... 25, 48, 79, 110

Geography 50, 136, 148, 168
Geological Engineering 132
Geology 64
George Washington University 57
Georgia Institute of Technology 58
German 98, 136
Gerontology 116
Gifted Child Education 153
Gifted High School Seniors 96
Global Learning Network 65
Government 162
Graceland College 59
Graduate Record Examination 14
Grantham College of Engineering 61
Greenwich University 62

H

Health Administration 81
Health Care 119
Administration ... 61, 115, 125, 140, 144, 146
Education 153
Psychology 61
Health
Community Mental 87
Holistic 96
& Human Development 95
& Human Services 45
Information Management .. 119
& Nutrition 50
Physics 146
Physics/Radiological Engineering 69
Promotion 81
Public 144
Science 119, 169
Services Administration ... 115, 163, 170
Services Management .. 36, 143
Services Training & Promotion 170
Henley Management College 64
Historic Preservation 105
Historical Studies 163

History . 30, 50, 64, 98, 116, 127, 148, 162, 168
    Natural 96
Hofstra University 65
Holistic Health 96
Home Economics 148
Home Study International 49
Hospital Management 140
Hospitality Management 72
Hotel Administration 147
Hotel & Restaurant Management 95
How to Communicate 32
How to think 32
Human Behavior 88
Human Development 51, 85
Human Science 106
Human Services . 41, 55, 96, 123, 161, 163
Humanities26, 33, 39, 64, 66, 96, 116, 118, 135, 139, 147, 148, 150, 160, 172

I

Illustration 122
Independent Guided Study 7
Indiana Institute of Technology67
Indiana University 68
Individualized Studies 91
Industrial Engineering 44, 58, 72
Industrial Science 43
Industrial Technology 105, 148
Information Resources Management 73, 74, 139
Information Systems & Technology 74
Institute for Advanced Study of Human Sexuality 70
Interactive Computer Courses ... 7
Interdisciplinary Social Sciences 84
Interdisciplinary Studies .. 55, 66, 79, 87, 114, 163
International Business 90, 153
International Consultants of

Delaware, Inc. 15
International Education Research Foundation 15
International Language & Culture 85
International Law & Business . 45
International School of Information Management 73
International Studies 153
Iowa State University 74
Italian 136

J

Jewish History 136
Journalism 64, 116
Juris Doctor Degree 88

K

Kansas State University 76
Kinesiology 169

L

Land Management 169
Languages . 50, 64, 102, 148, 160
Latin American Studies 136
Law 23, 64
Law Ag 76
Law & Rhetoric ....
Leadership Studies 163
Learning Contract 7
Leisure Studies 135
Lesley College Graduate School ...
Letters, Arts & Sciences 95
Liberal Arts .. 19, 23, 92, 99, 143, 148, 168, 171
Liberal Studies 60, 101, 121
Liberty University 79
Library Science 85, 122, 135
Linguistics 64
Literacy 85
Literature 64, 148, 162, 163
Livestock Housing 75
Loma Linda University 80
Loyola University 81

M

Magnetic Resonance Imaging 170

Man & Beauty 32

Man & Society 32

Man & the Meaning of Life 32

Man & the Universe 32

Management ..21, 22, 37, 64, 84, 90, 96, 115, 116, 123, 136, 139, 148, 153, 161, 163

Management

    Dietary 148

    Dietetic Food Systems 95

    Disaster 157

    Energy 157

    Engineering 139

    Environmental 136

    Financial 136

    Health Information 119

    Health Services 143

    Hospitality 72

    Hotel & Restaurant 95

    Land 169

    Mortgage 148

    Technology 103

    Organizational 151

    Pest 75

    Property 148

    Resource 127

    Restaurant & Food Service 122

    Soil 75

    Studies 139

    Tourism & Hospitality 85

    Turfgrass 75

Mann, Horace 24

Manufacturing Systems Engineering 103

Manufacturing Technology 157

Marketing 116, 153, 161

Marywood College 82

Master's Degrees 3

Mathamatics32, 86, 98, 123, 136, 139, 146, 148, 160, 172

    Finite 86

Mechanical Engineering ...43, 72, 103, 132

Medical Fields 135

Medical & Health Technology .. 19

Mental Health Community 87

Merchandising 170

Microelectronics Manufacturing 103

Middle States Association of Colleges & Schools 5

Mind Extension University .7, 58, 83

Ministerial Studies 31

Mortgage Management 148

Mount Saint Vincent University 85

Museology 135

Music ..27, 32, 64, 136, 148, 171

N

National Guide to Educational Credit for Training Programs 9

National Home Study Council 4, 5

National League for Nursing 4

Natural Health 28

Natural History 96

Natural Sciences23, 66, 118, 123, 135, 147, 150, 160, 162, 172

New England Association of Schools & Colleges 5

New York Institute of Technology 86

Newport University 88

Noncredit Courses 7

North Central Association of Colleges & Schools 5

Northwest Association of Schools & Colleges 5

Northwood University 89

Nuclear Engineering 58

Nuclear Medicine Technology 170

Nuclear Technology 99

Nursing ..19, 25, 60, 64, 99, 122, 123, 135, 136, 146, 151, 169

Nutrition 28, 148

    & Herbs 29

    in Natural Medicine 29

    & the Natural Products Industry 29

O

Occupational Psychology 136
Occupational Therapy 148
Office Administration 112
Office Information Systems ... 112
Ohio University 91
Oklahoma City University 92
Optimization Program 43
Oral Roberts University 93
Organizational Behavior 136
Organizational Development . 163
Organizational Management .. 151
Organizational Studies 51
Outdoor Education/Wilderness
Leadership 97

P

Paralegal Studies 116, 139
Paraprofessional Programs 4
Parks, Recreation, & Tourism 143
Pastoral Studies 81
Patient Care Administration .. 140
Pennsylvania State University . 95
Pest Management 75
Pharmacology 148
Pharmacy 23, 135
PhD Programs 22, 37, 43, 45, 53,
58, 62, 70, 106, 120, 135, 139,
152, 159, 163
Philosophy 32, 64, 119, 136, 148,
163, 168
Photography 96, 162
Physical Education 135, 171
Physical Science 64, 143
Physical Therapy 146
Physics 64
Physics Health 146
Plant & Animal Breeding 75
Plant & Soil Sciences 75
Political Science 64, 96, 116, 127,
148, 162
Political Studies 98

Portfolio 8
Prescott College 96
Probability & Statistics 86
Professional Aeronautics 54
Professional Arts 115
Professional Certificate 4
Professional Counseling 79
Professional Studies 114
Proficiency Examination Program
12, 13, 14
Property Management 148
Psychology 37, 48, 50, 64, 79, 87,
88, 102, 106, 112, 116, 119, 127,
132, 148, 162, 168
    Counseling 163
    Educational 153
    Occupational 136
Public Administration 42, 96, 105,
161
Public Health 80, 144
Public Services 123
Public Works 157

Q

Quality Improvement Certificate
85
Queens University 97

R

Race Relations 32
Radiologic Technology 123
Radiological Sciences 170
Radiology Dental 136
Reading & Reading Disabilities
153
Real Estate Training 146, 148
Regents College 99
Regents Credit Bank 15, 16
Regents External Degree 12
Regis University 101
Religion . 48, 64, 79, 88, 112, 162
Religious Education 81
Religious Studies 50, 98, 148,
163, 168

Rensselaer Polytechnic Institute 103
Resource Management 127
Respiratory Therapy 170
Respritory Therapy 170
Restaurant & Food-Service Management 122
Roger Williams College 105
Ruminant & Non-Ruminant Nutrition 75

S

Saint Joseph's College 114
Saint Mary-of-the-Woods College 116
Sales & Services Technology . 171
Saybrook Institute 106
School Administration 153
Science25, 26, 27, 32, 34, 36, 50, 168
Security/Safety Technology 91
Sex Therapy 70
Skidmore College 107
Social Development Studies .. 168
Social Sciences 26, 66, 76, 84, 102, 112, 116, 118, 127, 135, 139, 147, 150, 160, 161, 172
Social Sciences Agricultural ... 75
Social Sciences Interdisciplinary 84
Social Services 123
Social Studies 30
Social Work 64, 116, 135
Sociology50, 64, 87, 98, 148, 162, 169
Soil Management 75
Southeastern College of the Assemblies of God 109
Southeastern University 110
Southern Association of Colleges & Schools 5
Southwestern Adventist College 112
Southwestern Assemblies of God 113

Spanish 136
Special Education 153
Speech 64
Speech Pathology 135
Stanley H. Kaplan Educational Centers 14
State University System of Florida 117
Statistics 44
Stephens College 118
Submatriculation 46
Summit University of Louisiana 120
Syracuse University 121
Systems Engineering 44

T

Taxation 166
Teacher Certification Program 101
Teacher Licensure 163
Teaching At-risk Learners Certificate 85
Technical Communication 103
Technology 99
  Industrial 105
  & Management 41, 139
  Radiologic 115
Telecommunications 74
Telelearning/Teletraining 74
Theater 32
Theology 116
Therapeutic Recreation 96
Thomas Edison State College 123
Tourism & Hospitality Management 85
Toxicology 148
Transfer Credit 14
Travel Study Programs 43
Trinity University 125
Troy State University 126
Turfgrass Management 75

U

U.S. Deptartment of Education . 4

Union Institute 159
University of Alabama 127
University of Colorado at Colo-
rado Springs 129
University of Durham 130
University of Idaho Engineering
Outreach 132
University of Illinois at Urbana-
Champaign 133
University of Iowa 134
University of London 135
University of Maryland 137
University of Massachusetts -
Amherst 139
University of Minnesota 140
University of Missouri - Columbia
142
University of Nebraska - Lincoln
145
University of Nevada 146
University of North Carolina at
Chapel Hill 143
University of North Dakota 147
University of Oklahoma 148
University of Phoenix 150
University of Santa Barbara .. 152
University of Waterloo 168
University of Wisconsin
     Extension 154
     Green Bay 155
     Madison 156
     River Falls ....
University Without Walls ... 65, 66
Upper Iowa University 160
Urban Planning 135
Urban & Regional Planning ... 169

V

Value Engineering 157
Vermont College of Norwich
University 162
Veterinary Technology 19
Video Courses 7
Visual Arts 148
Vocational Education 43

Vocational Education 148

W

Walden University 163
Warwick Business School 164
Washington School of Law 166
Washington State University . 167
Weber State University 170
Wellness Promotion 36
Western Association of Schools &
Colleges 6
Western Illinois University 171
Woman's Studies . 64, 96, 98, 162
World Education Services 15
World Religions 32
Writing 86, 162, 163
     Creative 105
     Technical 168
     Theory & Practice 86